"With *Beyond Collaboration Overload,* Rob Cross has produced a genuine marvel. He shows why collaboration is often overused and underwhelming—and how we can enlist its power more humanely and strategically. This is an essential book on an essential topic by an essential mind."

—**DANIEL H. PINK,** #1 *New York Times* bestselling author, *When, Drive,* and *To Sell Is Human*

"Collaboration is central to General Mills's ability to innovate, serve our markets, and create a context where our employees can thrive. The research Rob Cross and his team have done has been critical in providing pragmatic, research-based practices that our leaders employ personally and with their teams to promote performance and well-being. *Beyond Collaboration Overload* is a powerful leadership tool for us all as we move into a postpandemic, hyperconnected world of work."

—**JACQUELINE WILLIAMS-ROLL,** Chief Human Resources Officer, General Mills

"OK, you're really busy. Why should you take the time to read this book? Only because it will save your work life and your home life. Only because if you follow its prescriptions you'll be both happier and more effective. Only because it's based on solid evidence from leading firms and leaders. Do it!"

—**THOMAS H. DAVENPORT,** President's Distinguished Professor of Information Technology and Management, Babson College; Visiting Professor, Oxford's Saïd Business School, Visiting Scholar, MIT Initiative on the Digital Economy

"If you're drowning in emails and meetings, look no further than this book. Drawing on a wealth of evidence and experience, Rob Cross has written an unusually practical guide to help you make your collaborations more efficient and effective."

—**ADAM GRANT,** #1 *New York Times* bestselling author, *Think Again*; host, TED podcast *WorkLife with Adam Grant*

"Every leader needs to study this book—carefully. It's loaded with insights about how to scale up your leadership and help others to do more while maximizing your time in the process!"

—**TOM RATH,** former Senior Scientist, Gallup; author, *Eat, Move, Sleep* and *Well Being*

"Never in history have we had greater ability to shape our work and who we collaborate with. Why do we so quickly give up that control and choose to endure careers in a stressed-out and reactive posture? *Beyond Collaboration Overload* provides the insights and resources for us all to proactively manage collaborative demands and invest in connections that help us thrive in both work and life."

—**HERMINIA IBARRA,** Charles Handy Chair in Organizational Behavior, London Business School

"Effective leadership and management both begin at home. And Rob Cross, a respected thought leader, brings it to your doorstep. To help you lead in an often dizzying environment of accelerating demands, Cross has compiled a set of best practices on how to make ourselves more effective leaders for our organizations, and happier at the same time. Only read this if you want to accomplish more, but with less stress."

—**GENERAL STAN McCHRYSTAL,** US Army Retired; author, *Team of Teams* and *Leaders*

"Employees are not simply bundles of skills that we can bring together in the latest future-of-work scenario to work as seamlessly as we think. They are embedded in networks of connections that when intentionally cultivated can be the difference between an overwhelmed, stressed-out workforce and one that is thriving—both on screen and in person. Cross's two decades of research in *Beyond Collaboration Overload* provides this much-needed road map, especially in times of evolution and change."

—**DEAN CARTER,** Chief Human Resources Officer, Patagonia; former Chief Human Resources Officer, Sears

"There is a very real danger of drowning in work collaboration. This will only increase as workers, leaders, policy makers, and organizations reinvent work in the face of accelerating automation, hybrid work, talent/skills marketplaces, and increased longevity. Fortunately, Rob Cross, my go-to expert on social networks in organizations for over twenty years, brings us *Beyond Collaboration Overload*. This must-read book is a practical, evidence-based recipe for thriving in today's hyperconnected organizations. Get ready to confront common fallacies, like the conventional advice to build large networks and collaborate rapidly. Replace them with proven ways to actually reduce unnecessary collaboration and cultivate the pivotal connections that support both performance and well-being. *Beyond Collaboration Overload* provides a much-needed foundation to thrive in, rather than endure, the new world of work."

—**JOHN BOUDREAU,** Professor of Management, Emeritus, and Senior Research Scientist, Center for Effective Organizations and Marshall School of Business, University of Southern California; author, *Beyond HR*, *Retooling HR*, *Lead the Work*, and *Reinventing Jobs*

"*Beyond Collaboration Overload* presents compelling studies and stories that show how too much of a good thing can be terrible. Rob Cross's masterpiece is packed with proven advice to help you, and those you lead, streamline your networks, meetings, emails, and webinars so that, rather than feeling frazzled and exhausted day after day, you will feel energized and be more productive and creative."

—**ROBERT I. SUTTON,** Professor of Organizational Behavior, Stanford School of Business; bestselling author, *The No Asshole Rule*, and coauthor, *Scaling Up Excellence*

"The future of work will require people to manage networks and collaboration more intentionally. *Beyond Collaborative Overload* provides a recipe for doing that. It's a must-read for high-growth organizations and provides a blueprint of what will be required of us all for the foreseeable future."

—**STUART HOCKRIDGE,** Senior Vice President, Global Human Resources, Align

"Ensuring workforce performance and well-being in today's networked economy has quickly become an organizational and societal imperative. Cross's research and resources provide practical and easy-to-apply strategies to help us all."

—**ASHLEY GOLDSMITH,** Chief People Officer, Workday

"Play offense, not defense. Far too often we get trapped by the always-on demands of today's world of work. *Beyond Collaboration Overload* shows us how to move out of this defensive stance with pragmatic actions we can take to reclaim our time and thrive, both personally and professionally."

—**JULIE LODGE-JARRETT,** Senior Vice President and Chief People Officer, Dick's Sporting Goods

"Collaboration is critical to individual performance and well-being today. Based on two decades of research, *Beyond Collaboration Overload* shows how people can succeed in today's hyperconnected economy by streamlining collaborative demands and investing in connections that enable scale and innovation."

—**TRUDY STEIN,** Executive Vice President and Chief Human Resources Officer, IQVIA

"Work is geometrically more interdependent and complex in a post-Covid world. This makes the volume, diversity, and friction of collaborative demand overwhelming. We know that more meetings, faster, is not the answer, which makes this book centrally important today. Cross's writing and research are always powerful, and this is no exception—compelling, reality-based storytelling of leaders figuring out what works, right now!"

—**DENNIS BALTZLEY,** Global Solution Leader, Leadership Development, Korn Ferry

"Most readers will immediately recognize the profound truth of collaborative overload, which haunts organizations and people in every vital modern industry. In compelling stories that bring each chapter to life, Rob Cross documents the emotional toll and productivity drain of collaborative overload and offers a way out—with the concept of essential collaboration. Practical and wise, this book is a game changer."

—**AMY EDMONDSON,** Novartis Professor of Leadership and Management, Harvard Business School; author, *The Fearless Organization*

"Academic research has provided very powerful insights to understand the link between peoples' networks and their success at work, at home, and in life. Cross's *Beyond Collaboration Overload* adds to this body of work through interviews with hundreds of successful leaders. The insights, tools, and practical applications throughout this book make it a critical resource in today's collaboratively intense work."

—**NANCY VITALE,** cofounder and Managing Partner, Partners for Wellbeing; former Senior Vice President and Chief Human Resources Officer, Genentech

"Rob Cross and colleagues' two decades of research in *Beyond Collaborative Overload* brings a highly actionable approach to improve personal performance and well-being in today's hyperconnected world. It's a must-read for anyone looking to reclaim time, craft a healthy social ecosystem, and create a sense of purpose, not only for themselves, but for their colleagues."

—**CAMERON HEDRICK,** Chief Learning Officer, Citi

"*Beyond Collaboration Overload* brings a practical, research-based approach to helping people perform and thrive in today's complex, interconnected organizations. It challenges the assumptions we hold about how large networks are needed to collaborate more rapidly. *Beyond Collaboration Overload* shows how successful people outperform their peers and live more richly."

—**STEVEN BAERT,** Chief People & Organization Officer, Novartis

"We often say collaboration is central to our employees' success and critical to delivering work in a new and ever-changing context. However, we also seem to use the word 'collaboration' for every piece of work. *Beyond Collaboration Overload* provides a research-based road map for employees to execute desired behaviors in the right way. It's a must-read for leaders, talent professionals, and employees at all levels."

—JAMES PRIOR, Global Head of Leadership Development, Novartis

"Beyond Collaborative Overload is the most positively disruptive book I have read in years. Grounded in two decades of research, the book brilliantly conveys how high performers are able to reclaim 18–24 percent of their time by intentionally cultivating their most essential connections. The results are profound: greater innovation, performance, and well-being. Contrary to conventional wisdom, when it comes to your network, more is not always better."

—MICHAEL J. ARENA, Vice President, Talent & Development, AWS; author, *Adaptive Space*

"For too long we've treated people as 'human resources' instead of 'human beings.' Employees aren't just a collection of skills that we can unite to work together seamlessly. In my own work, I've seen that what people need now more than anything is an internal network of trusted peers, connected, as Cross points out, by efficiency and purpose. Those networks can be the difference between an overwhelmed, stressed workforce and a thriving one. *Beyond Collaboration Overload* provides the insights and resources for us to proactively invest in those networks and connections that help us thrive in work and life."

—AARON HURST, founder and CEO, Imperative; Venture Partner, Social Impact Capital; and author, *The Purpose Economy*

"*Beyond Collaboration Overload* reveals the fallacy of conventional advice to simply build large networks and collaborate more rapidly. After two decades of studying more than three hundred organizations, Cross shows how successful people reduce unnecessary collaboration and intentionally cultivate connections that yield performance and well-being."

—**TED GRAHAM,** Head of Open Innovation, General Motors; author, *The Uber of Everything*

BEYOND
COLLABORATION
OVERLOAD

BEYOND COLLABORATION OVERLOAD

How to Work Smarter, Get Ahead,

and Restore Your Well-Being

ROB CROSS

Harvard Business Review Press

Boston, Massachusetts

Library of Congress Cataloging-in-Publication Data

Names: Cross, Robert L., 1967- author.
Title: Beyond collaboration overload : how to work smarter, get ahead, and restore your well-being / Rob Cross.
Description: Boston, MA : Harvard Business Review Press, [2021] | Includes index.
Identifiers: LCCN 2021010028 (print) | LCCN 2021010029 (ebook) |
ISBN 9781647820121 (hardcover) | ISBN 9781647820138 (ebook)
Subjects: LCSH: Job stress. | Cooperation. | Self-management (Psychology) |
Group problem solving. | Work--Psychological aspects.
Classification: LCC HF5548.85 .C76 2021 (print) | LCC HF5548.85 (ebook) |
DDC 650.1/3--dc23
LC record available at https://lccn.loc.gov/2021010028
LC ebook record available at https://lccn.loc.gov/2021010029

ISBN: 978-1-64782-012-1
eISBN: 978-1-64782-013-8

The paper used in this publication meets the requirements of the American National Standard for Permanence of Paper for Publications and Documents in Libraries and Archives Z39.48-1992.

This book is dedicated to my wife, Deb

Those who know Deb have gotten a fleeting glimpse
of the joy, kindness, wisdom, and strength that I have
been blessed to lean on for twenty-five years. Thank you
for all of your support—in ways both big and
small—through this journey. Your imprint runs
through this book and my life in ways that
always amaze me!

CONTENTS

PART ONE

BREAKING FREE FROM COLLABORATION OVERLOAD

T he collaborative intensity of work has exploded over the past few decades. With companies transitioning to matrix-based structures, products and services becoming more complex, and team-communication tools spreading everywhere, collaboration has become the one constant of global business.

Today, practically everything you do at work is a collaboration. When you attend your morning meeting, when you confer with a direct report, when you help the new person figure out the right expert to speak with about a project, when you page through your emails, when you pause to chat with a colleague, when you move from one webinar to the next while simultaneously addressing instant messages that seem to have urgent time frames—again and again, you're collaborating.

Even if you go off alone to labor over a contract or a project plan, you're making changes to a piece of work that probably came to you from someone and will go to someone after you. Although you're working solo in the moment, you're still a link in a chain of collaboration that may have started as far away as the board of directors and may reach as far as the company's frontline employees and clients or customers at the other end.

Collaboration is great, right? It allows companies to better serve their demanding clients. Employees can craft jobs that have greater meaning. And in general, social ties are beneficial—there's an immense body of research proving it. People with deeper and more numerous social connections have lower rates of depression, heart disease, high blood pressure, and cancer. They live longer. Research shows that even their cuts and scrapes heal more quickly.

So, we should all be reveling in our rich social work environments. We should feel energized, engaged, and happy. We have never in history been in a better place to use collaborative work to thrive and do things with meaning.

Yet today's corporations are not happy places. Many of them are plagued by stress, burnout, loss of engagement, unexplained declines in individual performance, attrition, mental health problems, and addiction—issues that cripple companies' never-ending quests for greater performance. We endure a volume, diversity, and velocity of collaborations that place an unprecedented tax on our time and brains. And we experience many stressful micro-interactions—caustic remarks from the new boss, cutting comments from a key account—that we rapidly forget, but these moments leave behind negative feelings that last for hours and days. We go home exhausted but with little ability to pinpoint what is causing our burnout.

Over and over, I see the collaborative stressors bleeding into people's health, families, and communities in truly disturbing ways. People no longer have time for the interactions that replenished them—neighborhood gatherings, civic events, exercise with others, volunteering, and just being present. The impact on health and well-being makes stress more than just a concern for corporate performance. It makes this a moral issue for us all.

What's going on? People love people, they need people, they thrive on social interactions, so why are they suffering? And what can be done to help individuals raise their performance and thrive?

A Search for Insights

I didn't set out to answer these questions. When I began working with corporations, I was there to help with things companies usually hire consultants to assist with, like communication, decision-making, and innovation. But I soon realized I was in a combat zone. The stress, burnout, and exhaustion I could feel around me seemed much more urgent than any communication or decision issues.

It was all deeply concerning. I heard not only about frantic attempts to keep pace with work, but also of the consequences in people's personal lives: divorces, estrangement from children, isolation from community, health problems. I remember asking someone who seemed particularly stressed whether there was something he could do to rejuvenate himself, and he answered, "Well, I *might* get a chance to go to church on Sunday." That was it. Over the years, he had slowly fallen out of activities, relationships, and groups he cared about. He was down to just one thing—work.

I hated seeing what was happening to people. So, the distress and frustration I was observing became the subject of my research. Over the course of twenty years, the research, with a group of colleagues, developed many layers. The team created theories and honed ideas by conducting organizational network analyses with more than three hundred organizations, most of them household names. (See "A Note about the Research" at the end of this introduction.)

Throughout, I have been privileged to work in leadership programs, executive retreats, and off-sites with some of the top organizations in the world. The ability to work with corporate members of the consortium that I helped found (the Connected Commons), as well as through dozens of leadership-development programs that I conduct annually, has been critical in enabling me to both develop the ideas and package them in ways that have the most impact for today's busy employees.

When I started this research two decades ago, I thought I had a pretty good sense of where the unhappiness culprits probably lay. I figured I would find the causes among such elements as always-on communication technologies, time-zone-spanning corporate initiatives, poorly planned meetings, and difficult clients, of which there seems to be an endless supply. These elements had been shown to be demotivating on their own, and I hypothesized that the combination of them may have been creating a toxic sludge that was permeating corporations.

But the findings of our research took me by surprise.

Discovering the Real Problem

The main reason for much of the unhappiness among executives, managers, and employees turns out to be not some exogenous factor like technology. Instead, paradoxically, it is collaboration itself—or, rather, the dysfunctional forms of collaboration that most of us fall into by default.

For one thing, we collaborate *too much*. I realize how that sounds. How can you have too much of a good thing? But what I mean by collaborating too much is that we're too eager to jump into, or be dragged into, active collaborations that might run better without us and that burn up our valuable time and energy.

I also realize that "we collaborate too much" goes against the grain of most organizations. The knowledge economy is built on the implicit assumption that ideas and decisions need to be thrashed out in the presence of the crowd. The aura of importance around terms such as "transparency," "visibility," and "crowdsourcing" is an indicator of the high value placed on participation. Need an idea? Brainstorm it. Considering a new initiative? Hold a "hackathon." Information needs to flow freely, we often hear. Silos need to be dismantled. In many companies, management has become an unending series of conference calls.

But the reality is that we're all flooded with unproductive collaboration, and we're drowning. A drowning person is in a state of panic. A drowning person is overwhelmed and out of control and therefore incapable of thinking through many of the things that need to be considered, such as strategies for long-term well-being and success. Moreover, a person who is drowning in unproductive collaboration can't take many of the actions that companies need their managers and employees to take. If you're like most people in today's fast-moving companies, you have a big stack of should-dos that you never get to.

Your inability—and your colleagues' inability—to drill through should-dos is highly consequential. Companies need critical masses of people to take time to plan for the future, to help others, to analyze trends, to rethink internal processes. Dysfunctional collaboration prevents all that. The system dictates your every move, and you're doomed to follow.

This book will show you how to rethink beliefs, structures, and behaviors and to adopt new patterns of interacting in which you collaborate more efficiently and effectively. Are you a first-line manager? A manager of managers? A senior executive? Then this book is for you.

Or maybe you are an individual contributor, managing only yourself and your own performance. This book is for you too: as an individual contributor, you should learn to conquer collaboration overload so that you can embark on a satisfying career trajectory. Whatever your position, by reducing your collaboration overload, you can reclaim 18 percent to 24 percent of your time, or about one full day per week.

Discovering Essential Collaboration

I will also show how to invest your newfound time in ways that can boost your performance and help you fulfill your potential while improving your overall well-being. The well-being factor is crucial. I want you to thrive not only in your work but also as a physically and mentally healthy individual, family member, friend, and participant in positive social networks. Work performance means very little without well-being.

Specifically, there are three relational strategies that can magnify your impact at work and make you much happier in your career and life. Those strategies are:

- Tapping broad networks early in the life of each new project while simultaneously investing in longer-time-horizon relationships for efficiency and innovation (which is much more counterconventional than it may sound)

- Becoming an energizer to stimulate a flow of great ideas and great people toward you

- Engaging in targeted collaborative renewal activities to build greater physical and mental well-being

Collectively I call these strategies—both for reducing dysfunction and building impact—*essential collaboration*, a term that encompasses the importance of working together as well as the need to reduce collaboration to its essentials.

I've seen many firms make concerted efforts to foster networking. They knock down office walls, create walkways to route people through others' work areas, sponsor employee clubs and activities, encourage group lunches, and implement online collaboration platforms. These initiatives, however, are based on the belief that when it comes to networks, bigger is simply better. That belief is unfounded and counterproductive. Often, bigger networks just provide more ways to get overloaded with collaboration.

I make this point to executives when they talk about restructurings, technology implementations, or cultural initiatives that ramp up the collaborative demands on employees. I ask them, "By a show of hands, who in this room wants another email, meeting, or phone call in your lives?" Of course, no hand goes up. After thinking about it this way, managers are often a little sheepish about their plans for indiscriminately foisting these new demands on others.

Time and again, executives acknowledge to me that in fact there's very little understanding in their companies—or in the corporate world as a whole—of what effective collaboration should look like. Think about that: companies consume 85 percent or more of their employees' time in collaborative activities and have no idea what impact this time has on corporate performance, individual productivity, or—perhaps most disturbing—employee well-being.

This is amazing, given the millions invested in measuring and understanding other dimensions of work life. Companies create cost-allocation and budgeting processes that are so detailed and complex they would befuddle Einstein, and they routinely insist on tracking employees' expenses to two decimal places. But measure the impact of collaboration? It rarely happens.

Even though we all collaborate incessantly from the moment we open our inboxes each morning to the moment we put down our phones and roll over to go to sleep, most corporations have no one in the executive hierarchy who is knowledgeable about collaborative best practices. To be sure, there are people who can throw technology at collaborative problems. Or consultants who can pontificate on the next best structure to promote agile collaboration. But these and other people are always shooting blindly, looking to simply increase the volume and speed of collaboration without truly understanding which aspects of connectivity impact performance and well-being. As far as collaboration goes, no one is in charge. We are all swimming in this stuff, but without the right measurements, we can't see it.

Surprisingly, even the most-efficient collaborators can't articulate what they do differently. Their own best practices are invisible to them. In fact, I've found that most people aren't consciously aware of how much they collaborate or of the extent to which collaboration contributes to or limits their success. People aren't trained to see social capital. Yet in today's collaboratively complex work environments, nothing is more important for us all than to become more aware of how social capital works.

In most organizations, therefore, the chances are slim to nil that you'll get a clear understanding of how collaboration is affecting you. Nor is there much chance that your company or colleagues will help you understand these effects. So, no one is doing it for you. It's in your hands. This is a game you need to own.

The work of the more than a hundred organizations in the Connected Commons consortium that have participated in this research is uncovering practices that will help you chart your own course, with significant payoffs. I will describe those practices, along with hopeful signs that things are beginning to change in today's workplaces.

But first let me orient you by taking you deep into the experience of a leader I've studied—a leader whose story is inspiring, but also, through no fault of his own, sad and wrenching. We'll meet him in the next chapter. Maybe you can see yourself in him.

A Note about the Research

The findings in this book come from qualitative and quantitative studies that, to the best of my knowledge, are unparalleled in their comprehensiveness and depth. Credit for this goes to the member organizations of the Connected Commons—a group of over a hundred leading organizations that have recognized the importance of this work for two decades. I am grateful to them for generously providing me with a researcher's most precious resources—time, funding, and access. In addition, this community of organizations created a context for these ideas to flourish through a culture of co-creation and exploration, combined with a relentless push for practical results. I will always be appreciative for and humbled by what I have learned from the members and other Connected Commons cofounders through the years.

Drawing on data from more than three hundred organizations over two decades, my colleagues and I have tied empirical results of network analysis to individual measures of innovation, performance, and well-being. The predictors of high performance mentioned throughout the book have come from many rigorous organizational network analyses (ONA) in groups ranging in size from several hundred to over 45,000 (for an explanation of ONA, see chapter 7). In each case, performance metrics were separate from the network analyses and encompassed objective data, including revenue production and patent counts, and subjective measures of performance, such as HR ratings.

In addition, targeted streams of work informed different aspects of the research. For example, as collaboration overload began to reveal itself as a core problem over the past decade, many member organizations let us use network analysis to identify the most-efficient collaborators—those who provided the greatest return in networks and took the least time. Alternatively, the work described in chapter 8 tying relational measures to mental and physical well-being was sponsored by a range of financial services, life sciences, high-tech, and consumer-products organizations. Importantly, these companies provided access not just to network data but to truly meaningful measures of physical health and mental well-being.

The quantitative analyses—and the relentless push from the consortium members to create actionable insights from this work—led to a subsequent series of structured-interview research programs over the past decade. One set of sixty-minute phone interviews, for example, included a hundred women and a hundred men in Connected Commons member organizations who were identified as efficient collaborators via ONA. The interviewees covered the full spectrum of knowledge workers, from individual contributors to senior managers, and clarified practices that enabled these individuals to reclaim precious time.

The findings in chapter 6 are based on separate sets of interviews: my colleagues and I asked twenty member organizations to nominate people they considered to be their most-successful leaders, and we interviewed 160 of them (80 women and 80 men). We followed this up with interviews of 100 leaders of successful project-based initiatives. These ninety-minute phone-based interviews explored career-defining accomplishments of these people and the role that networks played in their success. Further, after exploring their career-defining successes, we probed their failures to clarify what had been missing from their networks at those times. These rich stories and practices informed our understanding of what distinguishes high performers.

The results in chapter 7 also employed ONA to identify individuals who created energy, purpose, and trust in networks, and interviews defined how these people did this. We have consistently seen that people who *create* energy or enthusiasm in networks are far more likely to become and remain high performers as well as to move more fluidly in and out of groups. To define the behaviors of these people, my team and I would leverage the analytics from ONA to locate and interview the energizers and those energized by them. These combined perspectives led us to a rich understanding of how these people engage in collaborations.

The well-being findings in chapter 8 are again a testament to the Connected Commons community. Members pushed me to think not just about performance as a desired outcome in organizations, but also well-being. Again, these same organizations provided me with access to a hundred very busy leaders to explore these ideas in sixty-minute phone interviews. This kind of access to successful people on soft topics is difficult to get, and I am humbled by the generosity of the members to create a context that can truly help people in these hyperconnected times.

1

An Amazing Leader Falters

When I met Scott, he was managing more than five thousand people.[1] He started in his organization in a technical role and for four or five years led projects with a handful of direct reports. His rise through the ranks was swift from there, culminating with being put in charge of a new-product development effort that became the company's block-buster product.

If I could mention the name of the company and the product, you would immediately recognize both. The product was huge. It trans-formed how its customers operated, and it spawned derivative products that became big earners themselves. Over a fourteen- to fifteen-year period, because of the initial product win and the derivative solutions, Scott flew up the hierarchy. When I came in contact with him, many presumed he was in a final grooming role, and they believed he was the leading contender for the CEO spot.

My team and I had come to the company to help reduce time to market for new products, and when I observed Scott, I saw what his admirers were talking about. He was clearly a strategic thinker. As soon as he had gotten into a position of real authority, he had prioritized actions aimed at increasing agility within the three 1,800-person units he managed, all of which were part of a division that facilitated credit-card payments to merchants. He broke down functional walls by merging smaller groups into larger groups. He took layers out of the hierarchy to speed decision-making. He expanded the number of people who reported directly to him from six to sixteen.

This expansion in the number of his reports was a form of delayering: some of the sixteen people now reporting to him had formerly reported to some of the six who used to constitute his smaller corps of reports. Now, he said proudly, "we are less hierarchical."

As a consequence, there was quite a range in responsibilities among the individuals directly below him. Some, as before, were managers of managers, but now a few of the people who reported to him were in charge of smaller teams with specialized areas. For example, Scott's direct reports now included the editor of a quarterly newsletter on industry trends. This individual was not a high-level executive like Scott's other reports, but that was OK with Scott. "I'm trying to send a signal that rank doesn't matter to me," he said.

Scott also made it his declared mission to liberate information. "Originally, the teams here were set up to be somewhat competitive with each other and not share information and resources," he said. "My predecessor really focused on individual accountabilities and to a degree created a culture of fear that resulted in excessive internal competition." In trying to mitigate that culture, Scott created numerous dotted-line relationships and internal working groups so that everyone knew what everyone else was doing.

He also pushed employees to interact with one another. He created cross-functional teams and held skip-level meetings. "I brought together people who would never have worked side by side on their own," he said. "By forcing proximity, I got them to see ways they should be working together—and in many cases, people were doing fun things."

All these behaviors were textbook forms of servant leadership, and "servant" aptly describes how he saw himself. "A leader needs to do what it takes to support his people," Scott told me. Not surprisingly, many people loved Scott and loved working for him.

So, it was a shock when the CEO pulled me aside as we were heading into a conference room and said, "I'd like you to look specifically at Scott—because we're about to fire him."

Strung Out, Wrung Out

The comment was such a stunner that I had trouble concentrating during the meeting. Afterward I followed up with the CEO and dug deeper into Scott's story to try to understand what was going on.

HR showed me that despite the glowing comments from a few of Scott's outspoken direct reports, engagement scores among his employees were generally quite low—and trending lower. Worse, people who worked under Scott were leaving the company for competitors at an alarmingly high rate.

Scott's peers were grumbling about him too. A few times he had inadvertently become a bottleneck, such as when a potential project for a huge retail group in India fizzled because people couldn't get to him quickly enough. And then there was the initiative that he jumped into when the leader had to go out on extended sick leave; six months later, he was still project-managing it while waiting for her return.

When I looked closer, I could see that physically, Scott was wrung out. His eyes were puffy. He seemed distracted. Although he was engaged and energetic, his energy had a frenetic quality to it.

The CEO suspected that his faith in Scott had been misplaced. "Why is Scott failing?" he asked me. I didn't have an immediate answer, but my gut reaction was to be skeptical of the implication that Scott was at fault. Too often in situations like this, companies blame the individual, when the real culprit is a breakdown in collaboration strategy. As managers rise in big organizations, they are unprepared for the intense collaborative demands they face and are rarely taught how to manage these collaborations from a network standpoint.

Part of the reason for the lack of clarity in Scott's case was an absence of meaningful data. The company's engagement scores and departure numbers were detailed, but they reflected symptoms, not cause. So we took a close look at the information flow and the decision-making interactions within one of the three big units Scott managed.

As part of our time-to-market research, we were already partnering with HR to survey the top 10,000 leaders in the company and then zoom in on the 1,800 people in one of Scott's groups, asking managers and employees questions like "Who do you turn to for information to get work done?" and "Who do you turn to for decision approvals?" We were able to use that data to find out how many people came to Scott for information, and how often, and whether they were able to get what they needed from him.

Obscene Numbers

Our analysis showed that within just this unit, an average of 118 people came to Scott daily for information. Their requests ranged from big questions involving multimillion-dollar expenses to minor issues involving hiring for low-level positions or small capital-expenditure approvals.

This number may not seem to mean much on the surface, but to my eye it was obscene—that's the only word for it. For context, in an ideal situation, Scott should have had no more than fifty people coming to him every day for information—across *all three* of the units he ran. If our numbers held across the three units, he had *seven times* that number coming to him every day.

We also asked the always-revealing question, "Who do you need *greater* contact with in order to be successful?" We found that 78 people— more than 50 percent—of the 118 people frequently coming to Scott in that one unit felt they couldn't hit their business goals unless they got more of Scott's time.

This was another obscene number. When we see that figure edge up past 25 percent of a leader's immediate network, we know we've got trouble. Although the leader doesn't feel it while racing from meeting to meeting, he or she is slowing things down significantly. The leader starts to burn out, engagement scores drop because people can't get their work done, and attrition begins an often-irreversible climb.

We were seeing two distinct aspects of Scott's reality. On the one hand, he made a point of saying that he didn't hoard information. But on the other, hundreds of people were dependent on him for information, and many of them told us they couldn't get enough access to him.

How could we reconcile what we were seeing?

A Desire to Be Helpful

First of all, if you look at the overall evolution in management thinking, Scott was very much a product of his time. Although his company had started in the 1970s as a division of a bank, it had come into its own in the digital era, and like many internet-age firms, its organizational design was matrix-like, with many groups reporting both to functional and geographic leaders.

He also was an avid reader and espoused the current management teaching about the virtues of being transparent and inclusive. Scott was by nature a people person, so these virtues rang true to him. He waged continuous war against the tech-nerd culture that valued closed doors and devalued social interaction.

"In the past, when new leaders came in, they often didn't even take time to meet folks and learn about them," Scott said. This, he believed, led to intimidation—employees were afraid to bring their ideas and concerns to the leaders. "You can never build a real following as a leader by behaving that way, even if you're super talented," Scott said. "You have to talk to people."

So, he established an open-door policy and told employees not to hesitate to bring him problems and concerns or to include him in discussions. "I wanted to encourage a flow of information to me," he said. "I wanted to be seen as operating differently than we had in the past."

He tried to socialize every issue and use diplomacy and persuasion to influence outcomes. He was involved in nonstop meetings and conversations, throughout his workday and deep into each evening, as interactions moved from meetings to email.

He told me that once, lying in bed, he had tried to count the number of people he had interacted with in the past sixteen hours, a particularly event-filled day. When he got to a hundred, he stopped. He was impressed with his ability to talk to anyone at any level, and he felt sure that he was a paradigm of the servant leader. Though he was tired, and though he had gotten into an argument with his wife that evening, he still felt satisfied with what he was doing—at least in the work sphere of his life.

I want to emphasize that all of this came from a good place. Scott wasn't a micromanager, a control freak, or an egomaniac—not in the least. Nor did he refuse to delegate. He truly enjoyed being relational, partly because he derived a sense of purpose from supporting people. His desire to help was powerful and core to his identity as a leader. He felt he needed to show he was listening and was present so that he could demonstrate his worth and engagement.

In authentic moments, he would also say he loved to feel needed. This was, in a sense, a strength. Yet, in speaking to him, we came to see that this strength was also a significant weakness in that it pushed him to respond to every request, no matter how small or offhand. He was constantly coming to others' aid. And as people came to see him as the path of least resistance, these interactions mushroomed.

The sheer volume of the demands for his help was enormous, as was the number of distractions that fractured his days. Research shows that after an interruption consisting of simply looking down at a text, it takes us sixty-four seconds, on average, to reorient cognitively to the task at hand. After just a slightly bigger interruption, it can take us twenty-three minutes or more to fully get back to a task. And Scott was constantly interrupted, which meant he spent most of his day just reorienting cognitively to what he was supposed to be doing.

Making People Want Him

We soon identified an additional issue: in many instances, Scott seemed to *generate* a need for his expertise. He was extremely adept at this. Because he felt that he was only really doing his job when he was helping, he found many ways—some of them beyond his conscious awareness—of making people feel that they needed his input at every step of every process. He encouraged people to cc him on email discussions, which he would monitor and join when he noticed that problems or disagreements were arising. He believed he was being supportive by doing this.

At one point, he was paging through his emails when he spotted a discussion about a project to improve software for processing payments made through prepaid cards. He wasn't directly responsible for the prepaid-card side of the business, but the topic interested him and he knew something about it, having worked on prepaid cards at an early stage of his career.

At first, he didn't comment on the specifics. "Very interesting discussion," he wrote. "Keep me in the loop!" But when he saw people talking about outsourcing software solutions, he could feel his blood pressure begin to rise. Outsourcing, he thought, seemed totally unnecessary here. "A model-driven architecture with a really good template library is all you need," he wrote. "That way you create a highly customizable processing platform." His interjection changed the course of the discussion. Several people on the thread thanked him for the guidance.

As a consequence of this kind of behavior, people had become conditioned to rely on Scott's help. Whether they asked or not, they knew he would always become part of every important discussion.

Scott's "escalating citizenship," to use a term from researchers Mark C. Bolino and William H. Turnley, fed on itself: the more he jumped into projects, the more essential he seemed, and the more discussions he became involved in. He took on greater and greater responsibility for increasingly routine decisions. Meetings would pop up on his calendar as employees sought alignment, and emails would come to him checking on smaller and smaller issues.

But did he actually always know what he was talking about? Did he really have a superior understanding?

I discovered by talking to his team that a lot of Scott's ideas were ill-formed and half-baked. Yet because he was Scott, he couldn't be ignored. The team ended up with a double burden: managing the outsourcing issue and managing Scott. As a consequence of situations like this, Scott constantly added to his team's and his own overload at the same time.

But Scott never made the connection between his behavior at point A and the trebling or quadrupling of his collaborative work at point B.

The Tragic Consequences

What was happening to Scott was something you've heard about many times, but probably in a very different context. It comes from an 1833 lecture by an Oxford professor, William Forster Lloyd, about overpopulation, a pressing issue at a time when the number of people in England was growing by leaps and bounds.

In a discussion about resources, Lloyd pointed out that while "no prudent man" would ever put more cattle into his own private enclosure than his meadow could feed, the calculation changes if he uses a shared grazing area, such as the public common. The farmer might be tempted to put more animals on the common than he should, because he knows they wouldn't go hungry—they'd simply eat up more of the shared meadow. "If a person . . . puts more cattle on a common, the food which they consume forms a deduction which is shared between all the cattle . . . , and only a small part of it is taken from his own cattle," Lloyd said. If other farmers do the same, the public space gets overgrazed, and the whole town suffers.

Lloyd's insight, dubbed "the tragedy of the commons," is still relevant today. You've probably heard it applied to commercial fishing or pollution. Or you may have heard your colleagues muttering the phrase when the copier breaks down or conference rooms are over-booked. But have you ever thought of "commons" applying to employees and managers?

Scott was a misused common "good." People weren't "consuming" him well; they were asking too much of him and using him for the wrong things. He had become an overtaxed resource. His life was dictated by others' needs. This was bad from an organizational point of view, and it was bad on a personal level.

Creating Chaos

On the *organizational* level, Scott's involvement in minutiae created two problems. First, it slowed decision processes. While some appreciated his participation in the prepaid-card discussion, we could see how it threw the conversation into chaos. The originator of the thread tried to get things back on track by saying this was a side issue that could be dealt with later, but there was no stopping the unraveling of the discussion. It devolved into fragmented conversations.

Second, Scott was depriving his employees of challenges that would allow them to grow and was limiting the freedom that is a critical component of experiencing purpose and engaging fully in work. Scott wasn't micromanaging, and he would have told you that. He wasn't transferring pressure from above (which is where micromanagement often comes from). Instead—and this is one of the critical, novel findings of our research—Scott's desire to help and his network's response to that desire is what short-circuited employees' opportunities.

Because every problem could be resolved by going to Scott, there was no point in employees making the effort to come up with creative solutions independently. Ergo, they had fewer chances to show off their capabilities. They felt unable to progress through the organization, and their work was no longer exciting for them. Without realizing it, Scott was blocking his employees from following the kind of route he himself had taken through the company.

It was becoming much easier to understand why engagement scores among Scott's units were dropping and resentment was growing. Employees of a manager like him tend to experience high levels of frustration.

At the Breaking Point

This slow-motion train wreck was painful to observe. But by far the most distressing part was seeing what was happening to Scott's home life.

On the *personal* level, Scott was being worn down and used up. His upbringing in the lakes region of Minnesota had been idyllic. He came from a churchgoing family, was an avid athlete in high school, and spent most of his spare time hiking with friends. But after he joined the workforce, he found that between commuting, working long hours, and taking business trips, his physical activity fell off. Trying to stay active, he joined a basketball league, but he sprained his ankle so badly that the injury dogged him for years and led to further inactivity. The more he stayed away, the rustier and more out of shape he got, until he finally lost contact with the league, which was a loss for his physical health and for his sense of camaraderie.

He married and had children. Church, a big part of his identity growing up, became an insignificant aspect of his life. "I lost all the groups and hobbies that I loved," he said.

Then he and his wife made the kind of decision I call "the step too far." They bought a house in a better school district that was a longer train ride to Scott's office. The move wasn't a product of greed or materialism. It was just the kind of move a responsible provider makes. "You justify all kinds of sacrifices, saying, 'I am doing this to take care of my family,' and it felt like we could buckle down and make this happen like every other step," he said. "But suddenly I was getting home so late at night that I barely got enough sleep and would use naps on the train to catch up."

Scott kept trying to summon new levels of energy for his rising de-mands, but there was no more energy left. Brute force wasn't doing the trick. He didn't have time to rest or recharge. He couldn't find a minute to think about his long-term career goals, much less strategize about how to reach them.

As all this was happening, he began taking blood-pressure medication; he had become prediabetic. His wife became resentful of his absorption in work, so home was no longer a safe haven. One day she informed him, to his surprise, that the marriage was in a bad place and that she was thinking about a separation.

Needless to say, the outside stressors only added to his sense of being overwhelmed. Scott told me he had been having persistent thoughts of just giving it all up and quitting the company. His departure would have given him relief from the stress, but it would have wrecked his family's finances and would have been a severe blow to the organization, considering the extent of his knowledge and his networks.

Scott's diagnosis was *collaboration overload*. Was there a cure for this? Scott understood that his life was way out of balance, but his attempts to fix things by using existing time-management guides had failed. Most of the standard recommendations for time management assume that people like Scott operate in isolation. But we're not atoms; we don't work in isolation. We work in collaboratively complex environments; we are fully embedded in networks, which funnel work and collaboration to us at a pace and level never seen before. For Scott, and for so many people in my research, the killer was not one or two big things but rather the death of a thousand cuts from collaborations coming from all levels and all areas of life.

Collaboration overload strips us of the interactions that help us clarify and pursue our own priorities—capabilities we want to be distinguished by and values we want to experience in our careers. This is a widespread problem. Roughly 90 percent of the hundreds of leaders I have interviewed—successful women and men, by all external standards—described losing years of their working lives to collaboration overload. During these stretches, they frenetically worked eighty-hour weeks, feeling that they were doing the right thing, only to wake up one day to some form of shocking realization that, like Scott, they had been in an echo chamber—constantly hearing and repeating the need to work at a breakneck pace for financial rewards and a nirvana-like future that seemed to be perpetually just over the horizon. No voices offered alternative points of view on ways to live life or what is truly worth doing, until some jarring moment of recognition when people would recognize they had let large portions of their life slip by on autopilot in a way that was not meaningful.

Scott did finally find a cure. His problem was solved through an intervention that altered the *beliefs*, *structures*, and *behaviors* that had put him into this situation and kept him there. The solution enabled Scott to buy back time so he could make smart investments in essential collaborations that helped him identify and move toward his professional and personal priorities—and thereby grow and develop as a true leader.

I will thoroughly explain this approach to addressing collaboration overload in the coming chapters, walking you through the solutions by providing interactive "Coaching Break" exercises and chapter-ending features that will help you focus on one or two actions you can take immediately. And, in chapter 4, I will return to Scott's story to show you how it all turned out.

For now, suffice it to say that Scott, of all people, should have been the first to see the need for these solutions; after all, the effects of collaboration overload were becoming more and more apparent to him every day. The things he had put on hold were piling up and becoming problematic, and his performance was suffering.

Unfortunately, like most of us who find ourselves overwhelmed, he couldn't see it.

The Satisfactions of Dysfunctional Collaboration

There was an additional dimension to Scott's situation that I find everywhere, in companies of all kinds, and even in myself: Scott really *liked* to be pushed to the limit. He *liked* collaboration overload.

Until overload becomes a problem we can't escape from, we don't feel it as a negative. That's what's so insidious about overload: it feels good until it doesn't. For one thing, we have an aversion to not being fully booked up. When we don't have enough to do, we get concerned. *What am I doing here? Why don't others need me? If I'm not needed 24-7, what is my value? Do people notice that I have time on my hands? If so, do they think less of me?*

But it's not just fear of sitting around that drives us into super busyness. The reality is that the times when we're pushed to the limit can also be some of the most satisfying moments in our careers.

It's a great feeling to have every ounce of brainpower and stamina focused on a collaborative task. You feel certain about your contributions. You're needed and appreciated. You are energized and exhilarated by getting things done at a blistering rate.

The people around you are energized too. They're thrilled to see you at the top of your game, and they reinforce your behaviors. They tell you how much they appreciate your help and how smart you are. And they make it clear that they expect you to continue to be the hero every day going forward.

You don't have time to worry about awkward, uncomfortable, nonwork things—you don't even have time to feel *guilty* about not worrying about them. Your all-encompassing tasks block out all distractions, giving you that seductive sense of frenetic tranquility that we've all known and felt drawn in by.

I admit that I do this too, despite my awareness of the dangers of overload. I'm so driven by the need for accomplishment that if I see even a sliver of time—just ten minutes—opening up in my schedule, I rush to fill it with more than could possibly fit.

So, while it's true that the collaborative demands of today's knowledge workplaces are greater than ever, a big part of the problem is within ourselves. On a deep and often unwitting level, we don't want to free up time. We created the overload, and we don't want it to end. And people in Scott's situation, and companies like Scott's, are often completely unaware of the missed opportunities that are caused by collaboration overload.

I recognize, therefore, that my first task in helping you move beyond collaboration overload and into essential collaboration is to convince you that you really do need—and, equally, *want*—to escape from overload, and that the rewards of taking back a day a week and reinvesting it in essential collaboration vastly outweigh the satisfactions of extreme busyness.

To that end, I will try to show you the kinds of initiatives and achievements you and your company may currently be missing. As we will see in the next chapter, there is a world of possibility once you unlock from collaboration overload.

2

Why You Need Essential Collaboration

What is collaboration overload currently preventing you from doing? At one level, it keeps you from taking the actions that would help you be more innovative and effective in your work.

Personal performance and career-defining accomplishments are almost always generated by doing two things simultaneously: One, reaching out to networks broadly for help early in the life cycles of projects; it is critical to engage others at the moment when we are busiest and our thinking is most nebulous. Two, we must create enthusiasm and draw others to our work and ideas. As we will see in chapter 7, the single biggest predictor of high performance is the ability to generate energy and engagement in networks.

Which behaviors fall away when we are collaboratively overloaded? You got it. The ones I just spelled out: reaching broadly into the network for early-stage problem solving and being an energizer. Like a python, collaboration overload constricts our ability to innovate, execute, and achieve scale through networks.

But about one in ten of my interviewees revealed that they were working and living very differently than their peers—much more on their own terms than by society's and the workplace's definition of success. Their investments in connections enabled them to see different ways of integrating work and life, to take courageous action in pursuit of living differently, and to find greater satisfaction, purpose, and resilience in what they did. The benefits to themselves, their families, their friends, and their organizations were enormous.

Finding Time to Make a Big Difference

If your career is on a roll, it may be hard to picture how you could think and perform any better than you already do, so let me show you a few details of the work and life of one of those one in ten, the exceptionally effective collaborators I encountered. See how well you compare with her.

I met Anja when she had been at a global company for two years, in a job that was all about change and innovation. She had come to this job from the Netherlands, where she had cofounded and then sold a startup. Now she was part of a team focused on how people collaborate and the implications for technology.

Early in her transition to the new job, new company, and new country, Anja realized she needed to build her internal network quickly. She identified knowledgeable people who could help her, not just in her own unit but in diverse areas of the organization.

She began to recognize that the company was missing innovation and revenue opportunities because the consulting function and customer-facing technical support didn't collaborate much or communicate well. If an engineer solved a customer's technical problem, for example, there was no simple way for that solution to be captured, communicated, and reused by the consulting function—or by anyone else in the company. A great deal of potentially useful intellectual capital was locked up within the separate functions.

Anja discovered that everyone knew about this problem and had known about it for so long that they weren't trying to fix it. It was just an accepted fact. But Anja saw this as an opportunity. She wanted to remedy the situation and possibly go a step further by having the company package and sell some of the impressive solutions and knowledge that the two functions were generating.

Anja was already fully engaged in her own work. But she did not operate the way Scott did—she did not strive to become the indispensable helpmate for every colleague or team she worked with, and she did not seek to become the pivot point for every decision. As a consequence, she was not overloaded with collaboration, and she was able to take the time to persuade her network—as one among equals—to think in fresh ways about the knowledge-capture problem. This informal team, meeting first at lunchtimes and then on a more formal and regular basis, soon came up with an idea to apply artificial intelligence to the challenge. That would require expertise that the small network didn't possess. Anja said:

> Remote work is encouraged here, and I love remote work. I get a lot of stuff done that way. But projects developed in isolation, projects that don't get socialized with the larger organization, tend to fail. I've learned that I need to take time to establish personal relationships with people and teams in other parts of the company who can help us. That means having personal connections—really getting to know people.
>
> So to make this idea happen, I needed to build and leverage an internal network. The way to start is to have coffee or a meal with people and become friends with them, but we're in a separate city; we're not very exposed to the rest of the organization. We are not tied into any groups or business units. We are our own island.
>
> I saw that an internal company conference was coming up, and I knew I needed to go, because it would give me valuable chances to meet and socialize with people who would be able to help with the project. There's not always budget to travel to meet people in person, but I insisted.

Building a Network

Anja got the money for the trip and went to the conference. Her English was less than perfect, but she used that shortcoming to her advantage: she found that people were often willing to chat with her if she said she didn't understand the nuances of what was being discussed and needed someone to explain the terminology.

"I met people, I went to dinner with people, and I made new friends," she said. "At the same time, I found out what other people were working on and offered to help with their projects." Her offers created further connections and further cooperation: "They returned the favor and have been really helpful. They've driven the effort to get my project productized."

"In fact," she added, "the only reason that we've been able to pull this product off is that I went to that conference. I wouldn't have been able to do it otherwise. It helped so much that I knew this or that person, or that I had dinner with this or that colleague. The conference gave us the connections to do this work."

Anja was masterful at wielding influence without real authority, a capability that was entwined with her capacity to energize people and to establish a baseline of trust with an influential network. She created two forms of trust that our research over decades shows to be critically important. Socializing built "benevolence-based trust," or trust that you have others' interests in mind, not just your own. Her detailed discussions of technology built "competence-based trust," or trust that you know what you are talking about. "It created a sense of confidence in what we can do, that I am not just talk," she said.

Anja was able to disengage from the daily march and give serious time and thought to solving a significant problem. This is what the most successful people do: stop and think creatively, even in crunch times.

A year later, the new technology she designed launched internally, with mechanisms in place to "seek feedback to refine it and explore the ways it can be used," she said. "We have been working with teams and showing people how to use it and get them to try different things." The project is expected to launch to customers next year.

The moral of the story is that essential collaboration isn't just something nice to have. It's a *must-have*. Companies' performance and very survival depend on it.

The benefits for Anja herself were far-reaching. She got promoted, for one thing. But the intangibles were even more important. Her reputation grew, and a number of promising new projects came her way. These were opportunities that her peers weren't getting. She also realized that with her enhanced reputation and status, she got more comfortable in her own skin. She became less fearful of what others thought of her and more authentic in who she was.

In the hundreds of companies I work with, I rarely see essential collaboration like Anja's on display. In most organizations, the honest response to "Why hasn't your company been able to come up with breakthrough innovations?" would be "Well, ideally we'd *like* to be able to stop focusing on the distractions of the everyday and take stock of how the competitive context is changing and initiate a response, and we'd *hope* that the company's employees would be able to mobilize effectively, but we're all awfully busy right now . . ."

Anja is well aware of what assets she brought to the project and how she did what she did. Crucial, she said, was her personal authenticity, which others find highly energizing. She believes in being "transparent, open, and genuine, and not wearing a fake, corporate mask." She is not afraid to laugh at herself or ask questions that reveal a lack of knowledge. She will easily share something personal or be vulnerable with others: "It's a big productivity killer to not feel authentic . . . People who can't bring their whole person to work don't reach out; they don't feel safe; they hold back."

Effective collaboration—especially for innovation—builds on that openness and authenticity. On Anja's team, people are comfortable working together, being vulnerable, and taking risks. She never hesitates to ask for help or give feedback on other projects. "If we all keep to ourselves or don't want to show what we are working on until it is

100 percent done, then we are never creating great innovation . . . If you feel like you are stupid or it is not safe to speak your mind, it creates a culture where people don't ask for help or offer help."

Anja demonstrates what it means to engage people with what they are passionate about so they come to work fired up each day. Just as important is Anja's awareness of when to pull back from interactions and collaboration to create time and space to think: "When I have a week of back-to-back meetings, you can be sure there is not one creative thought that flows through my head!" So she sets aside large blocks of time that aren't dedicated to any specific work, knowing she's in an environment where "it is OK to take two hours to have coffee and sit on the rooftop terrace to think."

What Anja did for herself and her company gives you a sense of what you could do, what you could be, and what your company could be. Her actions suggest how vast your own performance headroom is if you are more proactive in your collaborative work.

But to become an essential collaborator, you must be able to overcome the factors that keep you focused on the distractions of the everyday—factors such as ego, reactivity, inertia, defensiveness, and fear—so that you can initiate innovative responses and mobilize people effectively, while also taking care of yourself.

Essential Collaboration Yields Well-Being in Demanding Times

Anja not only succeeded at work, but also felt good about her life, her health, and her connections to friends and family. Compare that to collaboratively overloaded Scott, on the verge of divorce and increasingly unhealthy. Well-being is inextricably linked to essential collaboration.

Insidiously, collaboration overload not only blocks you from making business choices clearly and creatively, it also prevents you from living a well-aligned life. In my interviews, I defined well-being not as fleeting happiness in the moment but rather as a sense that life is good and fulfilling. If you are experiencing well-being, you feel you're in a stretch of your life when you are moving in a direction that is aligned with your priorities and values.

While existing models of well-being acknowledge the value of relationships, that's as far as they go. They don't show how relationships enable physical health, growth, resilience, and a sense of purpose.

I take a different approach. Throughout my research, I have delved deeply into well-being's relational drivers. I do this because I know that if you're trapped in the echo chamber of collaboration overload, you're not going to be able to take in a flat statement saying you need to cultivate connections—you're just not going to be able to hear it or take it to heart. You will absorb this idea only if you truly understand the relational drivers of well-being.

Consider Dave. He worked for a series of startups after college, then accepted a senior software-development role at one of the world's most admired organizations. It was an exciting career move, and it made sense financially. "It was a big amount of money each year in bonus and stock options," he said. But the job took him out of the city where he, his wife, and his children had grown up and where they had family, long-standing friends, and myriad other connections to the community. Work quickly took over his life, and he became distanced from his family and community. "Almost overnight, I was pulled from coaching baseball for my son, being at recitals with my daughter, and spending time with close friends and family," he said. "What is weird is that it changed who I was. I knew this was not how I wanted to live, and quite frankly we didn't need the money. But the money was there and people all around me focused so much on it that I couldn't walk away."

Dave's story was a familiar one throughout my interviews. Often people have stark moments that wake them up to what they care about. For Dave, it came one morning when his wife gently shook his shoulder as he was sleeping. "I need you to get up and get dressed," she said. "There is a life coach coming to our home in fifteen minutes." This was a shock, but it had the desired effect. The coach, along with a series of discussions with a pastor, helped Dave reaffirm what mattered, and he began reinvesting in the activities and connections that had made him who he was.

In a short span of time, he left the organization and returned to the city he loved in a role that, by society's definition, was lower status, but that he has found twice as rewarding. He has never looked back: "This was a really dark stretch that I still reflect on with curiosity, to be honest. I had lived my life a certain way for a long time, had great friends, family, deep investments in a community I loved, and work that was rewarding and challenging. But then I got absorbed into the new company's ethos and perpetual focus on money, and I was trapped almost overnight."

The vast majority of people who successfully reinvent themselves do so by situating an activity in a set of relationships—in other words, they don't just do a solo activity, they do something that involves other people. Ideally, people maintain investments in two or three groups outside of work. For some, this means joining a running club (not just getting on a treadmill). For others, it means creating joint accountability to eat in a healthier fashion at work. For others, it means an intellectual pursuit like being part of a book club. And for still others, it means becoming part of a group in a religious or community organization.

Regardless of the approach to adding dimensionality to life, it is instilling the activity in a set of relationships that is key to the well-being benefits of essential collaboration. Dave focused on coaching baseball for his son, tapping a skill and passion he had developed in high school. And he joined an informal running group in his community and reengaged in a softball league. It took little time to reclaim his fitness and skills as well as to build friendships. Those first steps led to other things that brought him back to who he was when he was happiest.

Dave reflected on why the relationships mattered in each of these life anchors. "It's the accountability that matters, for sure," he said. "As an example, if I wasn't out there with my son, I would let him, the team, and the parents down. But it is way beyond that. You end up interacting with people from very different walks of life and learning how they are living. This opens your eyes to what's important and gets you out of your little bubble."

Dave's insight is a critical one that is too often overlooked. People who persist in adding dimensionality to their lives are not just getting rid of a negative, like an addiction or excess weight. Rather they are transforming through the interactions in those relationships. Connections like these can potentially expose you to people who share a similar interest in health, music, religion, or a specific intellectual pursuit. But they often come into the activity from richly varied backgrounds and so expose you to very different values and ways of thinking about what is worth doing in life.

These are authentic connections—you end up being vulnerable in ways that are different from what happens with your work persona. And you are present for others when they do the same. Connections like these are integral to essential collaboration, which—looking back to my definition in the introduction—is about not just tapping broad networks and becoming an energizer, but also engaging in collaborative renewal activities to build greater physical and mental well-being.

The dimensionality created by these outside-of-work groups impacts professional success on multiple levels. First, people consistently describe benefiting from the ideas and perspectives that these groups bring, particularly on tough personnel issues or thorny organizational problems. Second, people who do this well tend to be more physically healthy and operating with a degree of energy in their work that others feed off of. And finally, people with this form of dimensionality tend not to get caught up in and stressed out by the minutiae that exist in every organization. The dimensionality allows people to show up as more present and less stressed; they tend to be less reactive and less political over time. And, as a result, they turn out to be people whom others want to follow or involve in their projects.

A consumer-products executive said she decided to take action after an annual physical at which her doctor put her on blood-pressure medicine and told her she had crossed the weight threshold for obesity. She dusted off a bicycle that had sat unused for almost twenty-five years as work had taken over. "The first ride was pure hell," she laughed. "I didn't go more than ten miles. Every part of my body hurt and I could barely move the next day."

The next morning, she mentioned her physical misery to a colleague who happened to know someone else who was trying to get in shape. They began biking together with a third wayward soul, initially two mornings a week and once over the weekend. This slowly progressed as they began to set pace and distance goals and then joined a club that organized more-strenuous rides. Even through a cold winter, they maintained their rides "together" through a virtual platform: "Oddly, I felt just as close to the people—and maybe even more so—sweating in my basement by myself as we rode the courses and griped and joked. We all missed the scenery but discovered we could talk a little more when not having to ride single file."

By the next year, she had entered and completed her first hundred-mile ride for charity and had set her sights on even more grueling rides with this new group of friends. When I spoke with her, biking and this community had become an important part of her life and identity, and she had even traveled with her spouse and new group of friends to vacations that were entirely organized around biking treks.

"The group really has changed it all," she said. "Even when I am training indoors, I am thinking about riding with them or comparing notes with them. Biking is unique, because you pull for other people at the front of a pace line. The draft really matters, and there are days when I feel stronger and pull for the group, and days when *they* are stronger and help get me home. They see me when I am at my physical worst and struggling on all levels, when I am breaking down, and when I fail. And I see them too. It's that connection that matters. That's what keeps me going."

The relational activities that are a key part of essential collaboration don't have to be physical in nature. People describe adding dimensionality in their lives in many different ways. But whether or not these activities are physical, they pull you into being a different, more effective, and broader version of yourself. They give you greater stability in who you are so that you can more confidently draw lines to make sure you are doing what is important. One leader told me, "It is all these interactions—a sister who just came out of the closet, my small group at church, the parents of my kids' friends who all live life so differently, my over-fifty soccer club, an incredible diversity around me—that helps me continually anchor in who I am, who I want to be, and who I am not."

Dave and his entire family took a mission trip with his church, and it became a positive, life-changing experience. His career was none the worse for it. "It is amazing how work adapts to life if you are clear on, and stick to, what matters," he said.

As Dave's story suggests, it is not only the individual who changes. When you leave the echo chamber, family and friends change too, responding to your greater commitment to them by being more involved, inclusive, and engaged with you. If overload has taken over your emotions, your sense of self rises and falls with your experience at work, and those around you can feel that. But once you leave the echo chamber, relatives and friends come to see that you're more interested in them than before, so they open up to you more. They see that their invitations are less likely to get the brush-off, so they reach out more. They experience you as new and better company, so they spend more time with you. The interviewees who escaped collaboration overload told of their amazement at how much richer their relationships became. They hadn't realized how much potential had been locked up in those relationships, and how that potential had been squashed for years by collaboration overload.

This is not to say that everyone is quick to recognize—or is even *able* to recognize—the connection between relational activities and well-being. I've talked to plenty of people who never figured out how much potential is in their relationships or how that potential gets squashed by overload. These people say, in essence, that life is work. Period. And although they lament how hard things are, they say they would do it all over again.

Taking this attitude serves to protect their identity and how they have chosen to live. But what's really going on here, I believe, is that they have no clue what could have been. They have never veered off to explore new dimensions of themselves.

How Successful People Cultivate Essential Collaboration

I am constantly bombarded by journalists who ask—sometimes demand—that I tell them the one principle that will solve collaboration overload. But there is no single best route to attaining collaborative efficiency.

Instead, I view successful collaboration as being part of an infinite loop as reflected in figure 2-1. The first critical decision you need to make is to play offense by actively addressing collaboration overload in three ways, shown on the left-hand side of the loop:

- *Challenge beliefs* about yourself and your role

- *Impose structure* that helps shield you from unnecessary collaborative demands

- *Alter behaviors* to streamline collaboration practices

Engaging in persistent small actions in these three domains can help you reclaim 18 percent to 24 percent of your collaborative time.

The goal is to find the few practices that work for you. So, in chapters 3 through 5, I will help you clarify and take action on one or two items in each domain.

Once you've done that, you can reinvest your regained time in a way that contributes to your overall performance and well-being. This involves three steps as well:

- *Mobilizing a broad network* of connections for innovation and the ability to scale your work

- *Creating energy* and engagement in your networks so that opportunities and talent flow to you

- *Finding renewal* through personal connections that increase your physical and mental well-being

FIGURE 2-1

The infinite loop

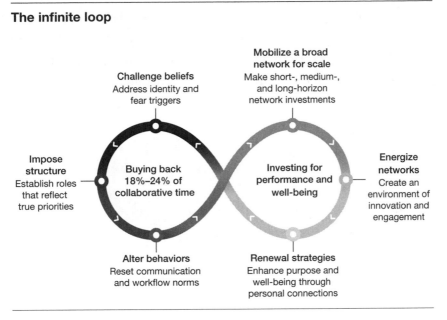

Challenge beliefs
Address identity and
fear triggers

Mobilize a broad
network for scale
Make short-, medium-,
and long-horizon
network investments

Impose
structure
Establish roles
that reflect
true priorities

Buying back
18%–24% of
collaborative time

Investing for
performance and
well-being

Energize
networks
Create an
environment of
innovation and
engagement

Alter behaviors
Reset communication
and workflow norms

Renewal strategies
Enhance purpose and
well-being through
personal connections

Ultimately the path yields greater performance and reputation, which in turn helps you engage in even-higher-value collaborations and so further improve your performance and well-being. I will explore the right-hand side of the loop in chapters 6 through 8.

You will see that each side of the loop reinforces the other. If you are more efficient, you are better able to tap networks for performance and well-being. And if you are accomplishing things of greater substance and showing up at work differently, you are better able to push back on collaboration overload.

I hope you also come to recognize the dynamic nature of the loop: this is not a onetime fix but rather a process that more-successful people engage in daily, weekly, and monthly. It takes time and discipline to regularly traverse the loop, to be sure. But it is worth the effort. If you don't take action on your behalf, who will? Most organizations do little to help people buy back time or avoid collaboration overload. Most organizations don't know how to provide this kind of help. When it comes to collaboration, the focus is always on more, more, more. Despite the increased collaborative intensity of work today—and the clear recognition that stress is at an all-time high—in all my journeys, I have yet to come across a chief collaboration overload officer in any organization.

This is a task that falls to us. But it is not insurmountable, and it carries enormous rewards. Let's take a look.

3

Challenge Beliefs

Put yourself in the shoes of one of my interviewees. You've been identi-fied as an efficient collaborator: you create high value for others and consume comparatively little time collaborating, as shown by network analytics. And what is your reward for this accomplishment? A ninety-minute interview with me—the flaky academic—to learn how you are pulling this off.

As you can imagine, the first portion of the interview, while impor-tant, is relatively mundane. We focus on how you use your calendar differently. We look at the nuances of how you run meetings or use email that make you more efficient, or how you coach others to use your time more productively. In general, it's a dialogue that stays at a fairly unemotional level as you think through practical tactics that make a difference for you.

But then at around the forty-five-minute mark, things change. As you get more comfortable with me and start to understand the depth of the issue, you begin to recall one or more pivotal decision points in your life. At this stage, if you're like many of the top collaborators I in-terviewed, your voice becomes more intense.

Your emotion level rises, and you say something like the following: "You know, Rob, I hit a point in my life where I wasn't healthy. I had fewer and fewer friends and activities I enjoyed. I was too distant from people I cared about."

At first, I get excited, expecting to hear that this realization led to a decision to undertake some magnificent act of transformation— hiking the Himalayas, sailing the ocean, learning a concerto, or going on some form of spiritual odyssey. Unfortunately not! Every time I am woefully disappointed with the modesty of the actions these individuals envision.

They thought they might leave work on time one day a week to meet with a personal trainer. Or avoid checking email from 6 p.m. to 9 p.m., when their kids went to bed. Or set limits on the number of meetings that could be scheduled per day. Or set aside reflective time to get work done. And so on. All fine ideas, to be sure, but not the potentially life-changing actions I was sure we were building up to.

And here is the amazing part: these highly successful people were extremely worried about taking these actions. How would others react? They envisioned a whirlwind of negative consequences: irate colleagues, disappointed bosses, floundering direct reports, scathing clients. But ultimately, to their credit, they chose to take these modest actions and await the backlash.

Then they chuckle in the interview and tell me that, in fact, hardly anyone noticed that they started leaving work on time or avoiding emails between 6 p.m. and 9 p.m. The few colleagues who were aware found ways to adapt. Those who weren't seemed to adjust automatically. In short, life went on and the world didn't tilt on its axis.

Clearly, in today's organizations, reducing overload is an intimidating idea. Most people never try it, and the few who do often become so consumed with worry about the possible repercussions that they limit themselves to only the most minimal steps.

What is so scary? What is the source of that fear? Is it peer pressure? Nasty bosses? Demanding clients? The fact that in the end, my interviewees experienced no repercussions suggests that the forces keeping us buried in overload aren't all "out there"; in no small part, they are also inside of us.

Whose Rules?

A decade of research shows that we create roughly 50 percent of the collaboration overload problem in the form of the *beliefs* we hold. By "beliefs," I mean deeply held, and often unexamined, desires, needs, feelings, expectations, and fears centered around how we assume we need to show up for others each day. Equivalent terms that I often use are "motivators" and, more often, "triggers," because these feelings motivate or trigger a tendency to jump into collaborations or to help others, when doing so is often not in our best interests or most beneficial to the organization.

Reflect for a moment on your own life. Think of a recent time when you were asked to do something and had discretionary ability to say no. The request was not for a project that you added unique value to, and it did not further your professional or personal aspirations. In fact, you knew with every fiber of your being that you should decline the request. But, in a nanosecond, you generated a series of reasons to say yes. Six weeks in, you wondered why you were always so busy and not living the life you wanted.

Countless managers we spoke with told stories of triggers that got them into overload trouble. It would be hard to itemize them all. The actual list of desires, needs, expectations, feelings, and fears that motivate people and put them into collaboration overload is nearly infinite. So, I'll talk about the nine most common. These triggers fall into two broad categories: those relating to identity and reputation and those having to do with anxiety and the need for control. (To help you see all the triggers at a glance, I've put them together at the end of the chapter.)

You're certain to have experienced some of these, and my hope is that you can apply the solutions the interviewees provided.

Identity and Reputation Triggers

Let's look at some of the identity- and reputation-related motivators in detail. What's fascinating about them is that on the surface, most of these triggers seem like good things, not negatives that will lead to overload, which is one reason it's so easy to fall prey to them.

The desire to help others

People find this trigger surprising because helping others is a core tenet of one of the most well-established approaches to management: servant leadership. But what's supposed to be a positive can actually turn into a negative. Scott, the leader we met in chapter 1, embodies the servant-leader ideal and, as a consequence, was always trying to help people— his direct reports, his colleagues, and his bosses. Yet, as we saw, his helpful contributions to discussions and decisions ended up making additional work for himself and others. (See the Coaching Break, "Don't Do It; Teach It.")

The sense of fulfillment from accomplishment

This trigger is another constructive quality and an important driver for many people's achievements. But in the extreme, this leads people to engage in collaborative work that creates overload. The small wins feel good. They reinforce who we are and provide a shot of dopamine. "I constantly have to remind myself to stop solving every easy little problem that comes to me," one CFO said. "Dealing with those things feels good to me and lets me avoid the big hairy challenges I should be addressing." To combat this trigger, this leader constantly questions whether he is the only one uniquely qualified to solve each problem,

COACHING BREAK

Don't Do It; Teach It

The daily choice about how and how much to help others can be challenging, especially when hands-on collaborations fulfill a deep need or reinforce our identity. Often, we get sucked into providing too much *direct* help and thus becoming the path of least resistance for others to get their work done.

- **Help others** become better consumers of your time, energy, and expertise. Do this by providing guidance that fosters independence and creates less reliance on you. This form of assistance can be every bit as satisfying and identity-reinforcing as hands-on help.

- **Be clear** about what kinds of issues you should and should not be involved in.

- **Provide resources** or assistance, but let teams and team members know they need to solve problems themselves.

- **Coach people** to be structured in how they approach you for assistance or input. Help them be clear on what they want out of a conversation. After the first five or so minutes of an interaction, ask, "So that I use your time well, can you quickly let me know what you hoped we would accomplish together?" This helps people stay focused on their goals in meeting with you.

- **Help people** see complementarities in their own and others' work; develop an environment in which others co-create outcomes and produce work in well-functioning collaborations; and frame their collaborations in a way that gives people a sense of purpose.

and if the answer is no, he looks for different ways to get the work done so that his attention stays focused.

These two motivators—the desire to help and the satisfaction from accomplishment—set up expectations in ourselves and others that quickly get out of control. When we continually intervene in projects, we expect those we're helping to respond, which adds to *their* workload; they in turn come to rely excessively on our continuing help, which adds to *our* workload. The need for greater accomplishment sets up the expectation in our own and others' minds that we will tackle every little problem we see, whether or not the result is worth the effort. This becomes an endless cycle of escalating collaboration.

The desire to be influential or recognized for expertise

In a quest for status, we assume that our role is to constantly jump into discussions and offer our expertise, even if it is not fully relevant. Others come to expect our involvement, so they slow their progress to wait for our intervention and adjust for it. Without realizing it, we end up driving work back to ourselves as requests for consultation pile up.

Consider Stella. After toiling away as an HR professional for twenty years, Stella is now a product manager for a technology company that sells HR-related tools. The product she manages is a cutting-edge "engagement tool" that encourages people to recognize coworkers who do things well or exemplify company values. It even allows users to suggest rewards for their colleagues.

Stella loves this product. It's what drew her to the company. To her, it enables what amounts to crowdsourced management. If your company implements it, your colleagues become your supervisors, your advisers, and your cheering section. It makes the old HR applications that Stella once used as a human resources manager at an athletic-wear company seem prehistoric.

Stella manages a team of fifty people who develop, get feedback on, market, maintain, and sell this cool new product to the company's existing customers, as well as to startups that don't yet use the firm's products. Things were going fine until another group in the company lost its leader to a competitor. The company didn't see a logical successor within that group, so a senior executive asked Stella to take over the leadership of the team, "just on a temporary basis," until a permanent head could be recruited.

Her first thought was that the task wouldn't be worth doing, that it wouldn't advance her prospects or increase her effectiveness and in fact would cause problems at home. Acting on this first impression of the opportunity could have saved her a lot of grief, but in a nanosecond of doubt, the recognition trigger got the best of her.

She had a vision of how amazing it would feel to master an unfamiliar unit with, in effect, one hand tied behind her back. She thought about the sense of accomplishment and the chance to gain status by influencing others.

All this was happening below Stella's conscious awareness. Her thought processes weren't deliberate; they were reactive and tied into her identity and sense of self-worth. She accepted the position. And she wasn't wrong about the positives. She tamed the bedlam and energized the staff, and it did feel amazing. She got that buzz of accomplishment and influence.

But soon she was also living out all the reasons why she should have said no. She was spending her days maintaining order in the unit she temporarily managed while traveling constantly to meet its clients. Her "real" job suffered, and she was forced to work untenable hours to try and keep up, but she couldn't. Her assistant, who always had an ear to the ground, said people were grumbling about her absence and lack of leadership.

As a result of her increased burdens, Stella had no time to invest in innovative collaborations or the kinds of informal networks that could lead to longer-term success. She no longer had time for her family or for healthy pursuits, such as exercise or affiliations outside of work. Her self-generated overload was crushing her.

The most-efficient collaborators don't try to get their sense of purpose and worth from demonstrating their accomplishments or trying to gain status. Instead, they get it from developing others and positioning them to become valued for their own capabilities.

This transition is critical; it is one that all efficient collaborators make to ensure that collaboration overload does not short-circuit their careers. In the words of one leader: "It's more about growing my people than growing me now. If you can grow people and keep them motivated, they're going to carry you forward because everyone's going to be successful . . . This aspect of my work was not natural at first, but I have come to love it."

Concern about being labeled a poor performer or colleague

This motivator makes it almost impossible to say no to requests. The knee-jerk response is to say yes early and often, so that everyone knows how competent and responsive we are.

When we get requests from bosses or others, most of us don't want to hesitate or be seen as complaining. So we feel that we have no choice but to say yes, and the result is that we get overloaded with collaborations. (See the Coaching Break, "Going beyond Binary.")

The need to be right (versus being able to find the answer)

The need to be on top of all of the details leads to a number of unproductive activities. It pushes us to spend hours preparing for meetings, digging into reports and figures. It may lead us to put a great deal of effort into writing perfect, bulletproof emails. Not only are these preparations often unnecessary, they also block others' engagement. They don't allow space for others' input. The need to be right also has a way of generating excess meetings and emails that consume many people's time.

Going beyond Binary

You will be surprised to see how liberating it feels to realize that a request does not always require a binary yes or no. To reframe your response in a nonbinary way, follow these steps:

- **Remember** that saying yes to something always means saying no to something else, usually something that matters, such as pursuing your long-term professional objectives or personal goals.

- **Ask follow-up questions** to fully clarify a request. The request may be smaller than you assume. Sometimes a few well-aimed questions can cause the requester to rethink the request, saving you hours of time. Create a two-by-two matrix where one dimension is impact and the other is effort. If the new request is high on effort but low on impact, ask whether there is an alternative way to meet the request.

- **Offer choices** to the person who is requesting your help. If the requester is a leader or client, give them a sense of status or control in the situation by asking them to prioritize what work should get done. For example, ask, "What order would you like me to get these done in?" Asking this question allows you to create visibility into the competing demands you are managing.

- **Set parameters** on the solution space. If there are two main dimensions of the hoped-for outcome, such as how quickly it happens and the quality of the finished product, tell the requesters they can push hard on one or the other, but they can't turn up the volume to eleven for both. "Just this language has totally changed what often was a contentious issue with some stakeholders," a software manager told me.

Anxiety and Need-for-Control Triggers

The following triggers grow out of worries that are so deep we often aren't consciously aware of them.

Fear of losing control of a project

This trigger is often tied into people's belief that they are the most capable of doing the work well. If you worry about losing control of a task or think you're uniquely able to carry it out, naturally you're reluctant to delegate or to connect people around you in an effort to form them into a self-sufficient, enterprising team. And if you're reluctant to delegate or connect, you sentence yourself to a life of trying to do everything yourself, which quickly becomes impossible.

Moreover, control-oriented people never seem to have enough information or a clear-enough process or a perfect-enough plan. For them, the easiest course is always to get more data, build more-thorough processes, and craft a better strategy, and their demands for these things consume hours of others' time. These leaders create churn and gridlock as the need for collaborative and decision-making interactions multiplies.

Need for closure

This need, which is closely related to the desire for control, can keep you on the phone or the computer late at night tying up loose ends in your email or trying to get that last little task accomplished when you no longer have the creativity or energy for it. Often these closure-driven communication efforts come out half-cooked, forcing others into additional work. For example, you might succeed in meeting a self-imposed midnight deadline for making team assignments, but they're so poorly thought out that they end up creating unnecessary work and stress for team members, and ultimately they come back to bite you. (See the Coaching Break, "Fighting the Need for Closure.")

Fighting the Need for Closure

Sometimes when I talk about closure, I get skeptical looks, as in, "Is closure *really* such an important factor in overload?" The answer is yes. Many super-organized people live and die by completeness, neatness, and getting things wrapped up, settled, and done—to the detriment of all.

- **Avoid completeness for completeness's sake.** It should not be the ultimate goal.

- **Give yourself permission** to have a cluttered inbox, to not answer all emails, and to not attend all meetings. Let nonpriority work or requests either wait or fall off your radar screen. People will probably find ways to adapt. One leader told me, "I used to go to every meeting on my calendar because I thought that was important. I have come to the realization that if they really need me, they will come find me. I am probably skipping 30 percent of my meetings now, and work seems to be getting done just fine without me."

- **Don't let a personal desire for closure** result in your forcing a solution too early. Value the tension of alternative viewpoints; an openness to information or perspectives may result in improvement.

Discomfort with ambiguity

This trigger often comes up in the course of a project when there are unexpected developments, such as a shift in the ground rules or the loss of an original sponsor. There's a seeming paradox here. People who are uncomfortable with ambiguity often cite its threat to efficiency. The ambiguity-averse argue, very reasonably, that uncertainty can create chaos; it's better to do the research and have the discussions well ahead of time so that all the details are pinned down.

What they often do not understand is that pinning things down creates excessive new cycles of collaboration. It can lead to significant overload, not only for the manager but for the employees who have to run around looking for—and sometimes manufacturing—hard facts in the fog of uncertainty.

Ultimately, of course, much of this collaborative effort goes to waste. The future rarely unfolds the way we think it will, as experience derails or reveals flaws in even the best-laid plans. The result is disengagement of the people who have wasted their time in the name of defeating ambiguity.

Fear of missing out (FOMO)

The fear of missing out on better projects, better colleagues, and better opportunities can become a persistent, nagging problem that won't let you rest or stay in the moment. True, career success hinges on an ability to create a marketable portfolio of skills and experiences, and as a consequence, many people—especially those who are just starting the climb—feel an almost frantic need to add experiences to their résumés. They feel vulnerable if they miss an opportunity to learn a new skill. *Was that my last chance to learn that skill?* They also wonder: *Am I falling behind my peers?* Social comparisons weigh heavily on young people as connectivity increases and social-media platforms allow for daily monitoring of others' lives.

Too often, FOMO drives unproductive choices to jump into new collaborative projects. Psychologists have long shown that we are notoriously bad at predicting what will make us happy, and we often overlook the downsides or costs of a leap. So, we end up in projects that overburden us with collaboration and that aren't well aligned with who we really want to be or what we really want to do with our lives.

The Surge and the Slow Burn

But how does all this happen? I mean, this research has focused on successful people, right? Surely they would be aware of and learn to combat the one or more triggers that get them into trouble. The ramifications are too far-reaching for them to not take action.

I've discerned two distinct paths that tend to lead to overload even when we should know better. Some people experience what I call a surge—they get into trouble all at once—while for others, overload occurs through a slow burn. See if you recognize your own experience in one or the other situation.

Surges happen when something big and relatively sudden ramps up collaborative demands. For example, promotion to a first-level leadership role or a manager-of-managers role is a crucible moment in which people face a quick escalation in the volume and diversity of demands coming at them. A sudden demand from a client can have the same effect. Same with a short turnaround on a request for proposal, a plea from an influential colleague, or forces outside of work such as a sick family member. Events like these drive weeks and sometimes months of intense collaborative work that takes time from personal and professional aspirations. Surges can be rough going, as we saw in Stella's story. But they tend to have somewhat definable starting and ending points.

The *slow burn* can be much more damaging than the surge in the long run. If you're experiencing a slow burn, you probably can't put your finger on when it started. It comes on gradually and builds almost imperceptibly. It is a product of incremental increases in the volume, diversity, and pace of collaborative demands. You tend not to question what you are doing as you add tasks and respond to the demands around you. You work a little deeper into the night or the weekend; you get up earlier to work through email.

And just as it has no clear beginning, the slow burn usually has no definable end. It continues on, year after year. People hang on and hang on. Somehow it's all bearable, until something goes wrong. At that point, the downward spiral is often fast and furious, and these stories usually don't end well. Victims of the slow burn have typically worked themselves into such a long-term frenzy that the relationships they need for resilience or well-being are no longer there. They have become unidimensional and define life success as success at work.

What leads smart and successful people to make the decisions that result in this trap? Any of the nine triggers we've looked at can be responsible, but the most significant drivers are the latter four—those associated with anxiety and the need for control.

Jonathan, a manager for a geotechnical engineering firm, was in charge of a months-long project advising on the placement of huge pilings needed to support a new, state-of-the-art bridge. His team's job was to analyze the soil and subsurface of the riverbed.

Jonathan felt that his firm and the construction firm as a whole were lucky to have him on this project, because he knew how critical it was to get the analysis right. A few years earlier, he had been involved in a similar project in which a few of the pilings were put in the wrong places and had to be removed, and during the removal process, the crane unseating one of the pilings collapsed, injuring three people. Having been through that experience, Jonathan could viscerally feel the importance of being accurate this time. In fact, he felt he was way ahead of his team members in his understanding of the project, his motivation to get it right, and his general expertise. So, he closely oversaw the testing of the soil and rock, went over the numbers super carefully, and wrote up many of the recommendations himself.

Jonathan also prided himself on having a precise, orderly, and uncluttered mind. He always tied up loose ends, he always completed one thing before moving on to the next, and he insisted that his crews work in the same way. "Get closure on that before you move on" was an expression he was commonly heard to say. For example, his project manager was a 3D-printing enthusiast and often touted the potential benefits of the technology in modeling riverbeds and pilings. But when he tried to demonstrate his ideas to Jonathan, the technology didn't seem at all ready for prime time. There were too many ambiguities. Jonathan preferred unambiguous methods that were 100 percent reliable and that could be deployed in discrete stages and whose output could be neatly tucked into reports, without any caveats or maybes.

In a high-stakes situation like this, it can be a legitimate approach to hold on to work, delegate only to people we trust, use only technologies we trust, and get closure on everything. But it can also create two problems:

First, fulfilling your need for control can lead you to cut off sources of messy, ambiguous information—in other words, it can create insularity in your thinking. When the data coming to you is limited in this way, you're vulnerable to being blindsided by surprises.

Second, holding on to work and delegating only to people you trust and using only proven methods can make team members feel that their autonomy has been diminished. When they feel that way, they lose engagement and a sense of purpose—and *their* performance lags. So, you've got performance risk on both sides: your own work and your team's work.

Jonathan felt this performance risk every day. He was aware that by stretching himself thin, he was vulnerable, and he was aware that his team sometimes seemed less than fully committed to his standards of excellence. He responded by taking on more and more personal responsibility for quality and performance.

That was his slow burn. To be the one personally responsible for the pilings, Jonathan constantly increased his collaborations. The things he was consulted on, large and small, continued to multiply. For years he managed it, which was all the more impressive given that he had a two-and-a-half-hour drive each day to and from the bridge site.

My interviewees told stories of managing the slow burn for astonishingly long periods of time. Some of them looked back in wonder—how had they survived? Usually they realized how unbearable their lives were only after a serious jolt of some kind—the loss of a key employee, a sick child or parent, a spouse who said, "Enough," or a project that took an unexpected negative turn.

Jonathan's jolt came when, worn down and depressed, he got sick and had to stay out of work for a week. He was wracked with guilt and worry about the job, but there was nothing he could do. It was as though that slow burn had finally burst into flame.

Meanwhile, the bridge site was being run by the 3D-printing enthusiast project manager, who, freed from Jonathan's strict supervision and constant need for closure, was able to spend some time creating physical models of the riverbed and the pilings. When Jonathan finally dragged himself back to work, expecting to find disasters everywhere, he had the pleasant surprise of seeing how detailed, complete, and useful the 3D models really were. It was clear that they would make the siting of the pilings an order of magnitude easier and more certain.

Jonathan was like a lot of the people I interviewed who were so overwhelmed by the slow burn that they were unable to see alternative ways of working and living. I remember one workshop I ran at a software company. It was nearly 6 o'clock on a Friday evening, after a long week and a long day, yet the session was still going strong, two hours past its ending time. The level of intensity was high. People were eager to talk about their overload and their strategies for fighting it.

We were talking about one senior leader's overload, and his colleagues, his boss, and I were offering ideas for how he could take action to reduce his burdens. But he was so caught up in his defined ways of working that he couldn't seem to accept our advice.

"It *can't* be that easy," he said in front of fifty of his peers, many of whom had been speaking from direct experience. He couldn't be persuaded. "Those ideas just won't work for me," he said. "They're too simplistic."

This troubled me. He was not belligerent, dogmatic, or arrogant. Throughout the day, he had been one of the most vocal advocates for actions the company should adopt. He listened to his peers; he listened to me. He seemed truly interested in getting to a good outcome. But at the heart of it, he just couldn't seem to see how.

Then this same experience happened again with partners at one of the world's most respected consulting companies. And again a month later with a high-powered group of managing directors at one of the world's leading investment banks. And then several weeks later in a program for chief operating officers from more than fifty of the world's largest law firms. It was the same dynamic each time: fear and anxiety had taken over, and these smart, successful people, caught in the slow burn, couldn't see how to resolve their issues.

But they didn't need to be living so reactively. The solutions to their problems were right in front of them; again and again, their peers would step up with persuasive examples of simple actions that could be taken.

. . .

Ultimately, Stella and Jonathan were able to constructively examine their beliefs. They saw that many of their triggers were based on unfounded fears. Stella was able to ease her internal pressure to always say yes to requests and demands, especially from higher-ups; Jonathan was able to let go of some of his need for control and closure.

But like so many people who are burdened with collaboration overload, they still faced the challenge of translating their revised beliefs into action. I will look at this challenge in the next chapter.

THE TAKEAWAY FOR YOU

Identify the Belief That Most Drives Your Overload

In this chapter, you've read about many different types of beliefs, or triggers, that can drive collaboration overload, but in the end, what really matters is which belief or beliefs have an impact on you.

Check off the one practice (or, at most, the two practices) that you see as potentially having the greatest impact for you. Then ask someone who knows you well to do the same with you in mind.

BELIEF OR TRIGGER: My desire to help others sometimes makes me too easy an outlet for collaborative requests.

☐ You
☐ Someone who knows you well

What it means and practices that you can implement

Helping is the quintessential constructive act, and it gives us a sense of purpose, fulfills a deep need to be useful, and bolsters our identity. But if you jump in too quickly or too often, you become a target for ever-expanding collaboration requests that bog you down and prevent you from meeting your bigger goals.

Develop an awareness of why people beat a path to your door. Is it mainly because you represent the route of least resistance? Learn to become comfortable saying no. Remember that saying no helps others become self-reliant. Shift your perspective from one of deriving satisfaction from directly helping to teaching people how to solve their problems.

BELIEF OR TRIGGER: My sense of fulfillment from accomplishment sometimes leads me to engage in collaborative work that creates overload.

☐ You
☐ Someone who knows you well

What it means and practices that you can implement

The bursts of satisfaction that you get from accomplishments large and small can be addictive, preventing you from focusing your energy where it is needed most: on the challenging work where you add the greatest and most distinctive value.

Practice avoiding activities that give you the rush of accomplishment for accomplishment's sake. Extract yourself or give partial direction while building others' capabilities. If you must engage in a small task, remind yourself that good enough really is good enough.

BELIEF OR TRIGGER: My desire to be influential or recognized for my expertise sometimes creates excessive reliance on me.

☐ You
☐ Someone who knows you well

What it means and practices that you can implement

The desire to influence others and be recognized can drive excessive collaborative demands. These demands leave you no time to invest in boundary-spanning collaborations or the kinds of informal networks that could lead to longer-term performance and success. Nor do they allow time for family or healthy pursuits. Expertise can become a trap of its own: a focus on your own expertise can prevent you from developing other people.

Don't continue to look for status in the expertise and knowledge that defined you yesterday. Be ready to let go of those old, familiar ways of interacting so that you can create the space to develop in new ways as a leader who enables the team to take ownership and engage independently in its work.

BELIEF OR TRIGGER: My concern with being labeled a poor performer or colleague sometimes leads me to engage in collaborations that create overload.

☐ You
☐ Someone who knows you well

What it means and practices that you can implement

The worry about getting a negative label makes it almost impossible to say no to a request, not only from higher up but also from colleagues—you may be concerned that saying no could impact you later. But there's a limit to what you can handle. Don't let yourself fall into the belief that you have no power in situations where your help is requested. Reframe your responses. Don't think of the options as binary—yes or no. Instead, offer choices, such as "What order would you like me to get these done in?" Create transparency into your capability and capacity and the volume of demands you are already facing. Then ask the stakeholder to discuss their true needs and see if there is a different way to accomplish the request.

BELIEF OR TRIGGER: My need to be right (versus being someone who can find an answer) sometimes leads me to spend too much time preparing for and engaging in collaborative activities.

☐ You
☐ Someone who knows you well

What it means and practices that you can implement

Whatever the source of the need to be correct—identity and fear are common factors—it generates unproductive activities, pushing people to spend hours preparing for meetings, writing perfect emails, and creating excess work for everyone.

It's better to admit that you don't know the exact answer but are able and willing to quickly find out. Establish this early on, at the beginning of a project or when you join a new group. By being authentic about your limits and having the courage to ask questions, you not only reduce your unproductive activities, but also create space for others to be honest. They can safely acknowledge that they don't have the answers either. All this increases others' trust in you.

BELIEF OR TRIGGER: Fear of losing control of a project—or a belief that I am the most capable of doing the work well—keeps me from delegating tasks or connecting people around me.

☐ You
☐ Someone who knows you well

What it means and practices that you can implement

Fulfilling your need for control can leave you overwhelmed with demands, and when you're overwhelmed, *your* performance lags.

Moreover, holding on to work and delegating only to people you trust makes team members feel that their autonomy has been diminished—and *their* performance lags.

The ability to get work done through others is a critical capability that managers need to develop and constantly remaster as the scope of their responsibilities changes throughout their careers. Draw a line between high-risk tasks that really do require you to hold on to the work and lower-risk work that you can delegate without concern. Letting go will help you build capability in others and free up your own time to engage in work where you add the greatest value. Celebrate others' solutions and resist the temptation to point out how you would have done it differently.

BELIEF OR TRIGGER: My need for closure results in communications (such as sending email late at night or making poorly thought-out assignments) that create unnecessary work or stress for others and drive future interactions back to me.

☐ You
☐ Someone who knows you well

What it means and practices that you can implement

An overemphasis on completeness for completeness's sake creates unnecessary stress for your team members and may send them off chasing unclear objectives that don't align with the team's overall work. The need for closure pushes you to try to force solutions, which has a negative impact on project success and increases downstream collaborative demands.

Remind yourself that closure—or an empty email inbox—should not be a priority aim. Don't answer all emails. Let nonpriority work or requests either wait or slide off your radar screen altogether. Do you attend every meeting on your calendar? The reality is that they're not equally important. Get in the habit of skipping those where your input isn't needed and see if people notice.

BELIEF OR TRIGGER: My discomfort with ambiguity and managing adaptation as a project unfolds results in excessive collaborative work to overly perfect or obtain buy-in for a plan.

☐ You

☐ Someone who knows you well

What it means and practices that you can implement

The most ambiguity-averse people never have enough information or a clear-enough process or a perfect-enough plan. For them, the easiest course is always to get more data, more-thorough processes, and a better strategy, and their demands for these things consume hours of others' time. These managers create churn and gridlock as the need for collaborative and decision-making interactions multiplies.

The most-efficient collaborators have an expansive tolerance for ambiguity. They don't need to have everything specified and pinned down, especially in early stages of projects. They focus on being *directionally correct*, meaning that they make sure they are moving in generally the right direction on the project, and they remain open to adapting their ideas and plans as new information comes in. Push yourself to make a decision in the face of ambiguity. Look to produce a solution in twenty minutes that helps move a plan ahead, rather than spending three hours and consuming others' time to get to a more accurate solution or employ a more thorough process.

BELIEF OR TRIGGER: Fear of missing out (FOMO) results in my engaging in collaborative work that creates overload.

☐ You

☐ Someone who knows you well

What it means and practices that you can implement

Too often, FOMO drives unproductive choices to jump into new collaborative projects. You may end up in projects that overburden you with collaboration and that aren't well aligned with who you really want to be or what you really want to do with your life.

Before jumping into a new project, make sure that your plans aren't driven by an emotional, knee-jerk reaction based on fear or social comparison. Cultivate relationships in your network with people who know you well and can provide advice that is based on who you really are. Bring people with a broader scope of responsibilities into your network. Tap these people to develop a counter-narrative that might help you avoid making a decision based on FOMO rather than doing what is truly best for you.

4

Impose New Structure

How did yesterday unfold for you? Did you spend your day doing work that you added value to, and that added value to you? Was it work that generated progress toward your and the organization's most important goals? On a scale of one to ten, how would you rate your day? Was it a ten? Or, deep down, do you feel that was it more like a one?

The paradox here is that many of us have a lot of say in the work we do. Whether we are managers or employees, we have a degree of freedom that earlier generations would have envied. As more and more companies recognize the power of autonomy to motivate people and unleash creativity, we're able to make many choices about what work we do, which aspect of projects we focus on, and who we collaborate with. Organizations have become competitive marketplaces of ideas where bold initiatives are springboards to promotions. Fewer and fewer of us are simply given a wrench and told which nut to turn.

And yet in many ways, we might as well be stuck in the old days of the industrial efficiency movement, when the starched-collar management guru Frederick Winslow Taylor, also an Olympic golfer, saw workers as little balls to be swatted around corporations with maximum force for maximum efficiency.

Why do we consistently end up getting pulled into collaborative work that has nothing to do with where we want to go in our careers or who we want to be? It's as though some invisible force were dictating our work to us and continually knocking us off paths we would prefer to be traversing.

The purpose of the previous chapter was to show that this invisible force is partly a product of our own unarticulated needs, emotions, and motivations—in other words, that the things that happen to us are actually, in large part, things we do to ourselves. The purpose of this chapter is to show that there are structural solutions to this problem that can free us from being strong-armed by the system so that, instead, we can take control and shape the system to our needs.

"Control" is a complicated and loaded word. In the previous chapter, we saw how fear of losing control can be a trigger that gets us into collaboration overload. We saw that managers who are obsessed with control can create vast amounts of churn in the workplace. But that is not the kind of control I mean. I'm not talking about the need to do everything yourself.

Instead, I'm talking about knowing where you want to go, for yourself and the organization, and making sure that you keep progressing in that direction—making sure that collaboration overload doesn't turn your life into a *Groundhog Day* nightmare of waking up every day in exactly the same place.

"What Was I Doing?"

Let's get back to Scott, the struggling leader we met in chapter 1. Scott provides a good example of the use of structure to alleviate overload. When I met him, the organizational network analysis we had conducted on the top 10,000 people in his organization showed that he was the number-one most overloaded person. By working with him, my colleagues and I were able to move him down to number seventeen, and then to number twenty-three. The process ultimately reframed his role and positioned him in work streams where he added unique value. As described in chapter 1, part of his reinvention involved altering his view of what it means to be a servant leader. He came to understand that it was better to help people develop their own capabilities than to directly assist them. Another big part of it was looking at structural elements of his work life.

It started with the company's response to Scott's physical health. He was wrung out and struggling on many physical fronts. So, the company took an action I did not know was possible: it sent him to a ten-day health and wellness retreat. The critical part was that the retreat unplugged him. He had to give up his devices—that's *devices*, plural. He describes the first day offline as being like heroin withdrawal. And to some degree, we know this is not too far off—neuroscience shows us that the jolts we get from continually checking our devices entrain us into a vicious cycle.

Somehow Scott managed to fight through the ten days, doing yoga, meditating, and not using his devices. But on day eleven, he was back on email. Ten days of messages had piled up. He had thousands of them, and he was determined to get caught up.

Diving back into his emails led to his greatest epiphany, a learning that has held to this day. He jumped into the email threads with renewed vigor from the respite. As he began to see issues emerge, he viscerally felt his body react. His pulse rose. His face flushed. He could feel his blood pressure rising as he thought, "I need to get into this." But then he would follow the threads over the days up to the present and realize—to his amazement—that many of the issues had been settled without him. Most were resolved within an hour or two after the point where he would have jumped in to "help."

He worked with a coach who pointed out, via feedback from direct reports and colleagues, that not only were these issues resolved without his input, they were resolved faster—and typically better—than if he had been involved. "What was I doing?" he asked, shaking his head. "My well-intentioned impact of jumping in was causing bigger problems."

Scott went back four months into his calendar to review his collaborations. He soon saw, in analyzing his day-by-day interactions, that his desire to be helpful wasn't the only cause of his problems. In a number of cases, the cause was the corporate penchant for creating bureaucracy. Routine decisions often become embedded in time-consuming processes because somewhere back in the mists of time, someone made an error, such as delivering a flawed product to an important customer, and the response was to create a policy, process, or procedure to ensure this *never* happens again. But typically, these solutions to a one-off mistake ended up consuming enormous amounts of collaborative time. Scott's calendar was full of interactions tied to policies, processes, and procedures like that.

The four-month time frame that he examined was critical. You can't look back just one week; if you do, you'll be so close to the issues that you'll see everything as completely justified. But when people get some distance, they are always surprised by the range of nonessential collaborations they are pulled into, usually because these things have somehow become part of the structure of their roles through others' expectations.

Scott scanned through each day on his calendar, looking for recurring activities or meetings. He was able to identify many opportunities where his time burden could have been reduced by shifting decision thresholds or roles or creating alternative go-to people.

Then he looked *forward* two months, scanning for the same kinds of recurring meetings and nonvalue-added activity. He was sickened by what he saw. There were many planned interactions in which he would clearly add no value, yet his participation had been built into the fabric of how work was done. For most of the items embedded in his calendar, his role was not to provide ideas, vision, or inspiration, but to coordinate work that others could have coordinated, or simply to be present so that people who lacked confidence to act independently could reassure themselves that they weren't making mistakes.

Using the Calendar Strategically

Scott recognized that he needed to put his *North Star objectives*—capabilities he wanted to deploy in his work and values he wanted to live through his career—front and center, and that in light of those objectives, he would have to rethink what decisions and informational requests he needed to participate in, whether portions of his role should go to others, and whether he could reduce his meeting time. He would have to be proactive about structuring his professional life more intentionally through his calendar.

North Star objectives

Scott reflected on what his true goals were for his life and his work. Long ago, he had been clear about what drew him to this company: his sense that the company's size, reach, and visionary leadership uniquely positioned it to provide tools to help the working poor and new immigrants begin to use the banking system. Many of the initiatives that Scott had been involved with were aimed at the "unbanked" and people with bad credit, helping them save money, transfer funds, and use ATMs. His work, he felt, had the potential to make the world a better place. That was important to him.

He had gotten too far away from all that—now his days seemed to be all about the minutiae—so he resolved to refocus himself on the "why" of his work. "Being clear on the values I wanted to live through work was simple," he said, "but it had a profound effect on how I started prioritizing and eliminating interactions."

Decisions and informational requests

He also saw that his decision threshold was too low: he was willing, even eager, to pass judgment on issues that other managers at his level would have considered too trivial to merit their time. In order to get out of collaboration overload—as well as to provide others with a greater sense of autonomy and engagement—Scott reset his threshold, at least for certain kinds of decisions. He stopped getting involved in travel approvals, for example, as well as human resources decisions for people who were so far down the hierarchy that he had never even met them. As he looked at each decision, he asked himself: Could a colleague handle this?

He found many requests for information that shouldn't have been directed at him. He discovered that a significant number were from past colleagues seeking his technical knowledge in areas, such as prepaid cards, that were ancient history for him now and didn't benefit him anymore. He realized he had probably tacitly encouraged these queries because he enjoyed being helpful to, and held in high regard by, his old coworkers. But no more—spending his time on things like that didn't benefit him or the company. Stepping back, he was able to parse the informational requests into various categories and then named an emerging talent who was more current on the topic areas as a go-to person for each group of requests.

Role

With his new lens, Scott began to question parts of his role. He took an experimental approach: "Some things I just stopped doing, and waited to see what would happen," he said. "If I got one or two emails asking why I was missing a meeting, I just ignored them and life went on and adjusted around me. Only when I kept getting urgent requests did I look further into them to see if I was truly needed."

In situations where he was indeed playing an important role, he looked to shift as much as possible to less-overwhelmed people. In the past, he had been told by coaches and senior executives that he needed to delegate more, but he had responded by shifting responsibilities to the one person he already relied on most heavily—in other words, to the next-busiest person in his area. That person quickly became overloaded, and the responsibilities bounced back to Scott. This time he identified people who could learn to handle big chunks of his responsibilities without routing them back to him. Equally important, these were people he was trying to cultivate and slingshot into the kinds of work where they could improve their productivity, become resources for everyone, and further balance collaborative demands throughout the system.

Meeting time

Scott looked at the length of each recurring meeting and asked himself if it could be cut in half. He also identified meetings that could be scheduled less frequently or, in some cases, canceled.

Pulling the whole picture together, Scott created what he called a "strategic calendaring" regimen. He looked ahead at each coming week, as well as at the coming four weeks, and tried to make sure all his activities were aligned with his goals. He scouted to see where nonessential collaborations were sneaking onto his schedule. He made a plan to connect the people around him and develop capabilities in his team. And he set aside time for reflection.

All these actions involved being proactive and refusing to cede control to the invisible forces of collaboration overload. None of the steps were particularly difficult, yet they had a huge effect on both his career and his marriage. "I was able to build more regenerating interactions into my life," he said.

Pursuing his goals gave him new energy. "I made sure that I built interactions into my schedule that matched up with values I wanted to experience in my career and my life," Scott said. "For me, these included developmental interactions and ones that were creative and involved plotting the company's future."

Scott was surprised at how little pushback he got. On the length of his meetings, for example, he said, "Humans can expand activities to fill meeting time like nobody's business. When I did the reverse and shrank the meetings, I didn't get a single complaint!"

I've heard so many stories like Scott's. Over and over, the efficient collaborators I interviewed told me how they escaped from meaningless interactions. In the next section of this chapter, I'll call out their most common structural practices for overcoming overload and engaging in essential collaboration. These practices can be grouped into two areas: the first are about orienting networks to North Star objectives, and the next are about shaping role interdependencies to improve collaborative efficiency. Let's look at each group in turn.

Orienting Networks to North Star Objectives

In order to feel confident about which collaborative tasks are right for you and which to avoid, you need to have a clear idea of what really matters to you. What are your North Star objectives? I'm talking about not just a single goal such as getting a promotion to a specific position, but a combination of *expertise*, *values*, and *identity*.

I realize that sounds abstract, so I'll get more specific (and, again, please take a look at the end of the chapter for a summary view of these practices).

Focus on your expertise

Reflect on capabilities that you want to develop, be known for, and grow into during the coming five years. Focus on the kinds of expertise you enjoy using, rather than on the demands of a specific role or function. This area of expertise might already be a strength for you, or it might be aspirational. Either way, it must be something that you enjoy, or would enjoy, deploying. It should also provide significant value for the organization.

That's a lot to unpack: What area of expertise, which you enjoy deploying and in which you are or wish to be strong and which adds a lot of value to the organization, would you like to see become a distinguishing feature of your work?

There are several diagnostics that can help you figure this out, such as Gallup's CliftonStrengths (formerly StrengthsFinder) or Donald Super's Work Values Inventory. An example might be expertise in connecting people. Let's say you really enjoy linking people with similar interests across silos, and you're good at it. You know it's beneficial to your company, but so far you haven't been able to do it much because you're stuck in work that doesn't make use of this talent. Defining your North Star objective might mean developing a clear sense that you want to become known and respected—and promoted and compensated—for this talent.

Defining a North Star objective in this way—and not with a focus on a role or promotion—is critical to the reputation you develop and to influencing networks to draw you into satisfying, purposeful work.

Focus on your values

What do you truly value? Be honest: Is it material items? Accomplishment? Creativity? Helping others? Don't aim too intently at specific roles. And focus on what *you* care about, not what culture or social media tells you is important.

Think about times when you were thriving in your work—showing up fully engaged and absorbed in what you were doing. Identify aspects of the work you found meaningful. Then characterize the nature of interactions you had with your network at this time that mattered to you. Did you love the co-creation aspect of it? Did you love working with people who cared about similar aspects of the task? Did you love the humor in the work environment? (Yes, humor is an important value too.)

Focus on your identity

What are the personal, outside aspirations and commitments that you want to hold true to? The list might include family or community involvement. Or it might include exercise. Is your identity that you are a civic-minded person? An activist? Fighter? Athlete? Provider? Caregiver?

These aspirations and commitments help you create boundaries around work and implement buffering strategies such as specific rules around when you will answer email, check texts or phone messages, and leave the office. They will also help you make what I call network-anchoring investments—investments of time with at least one and usually two groups of people outside of work that pull you into different domains and help you value things more broadly than work (I will say much more about these anchoring investments in chapter 8).

Once you have defined a North Star objective on the basis of your expertise, values, and identity, you can focus on the practices that successful collaborators employ to reach their objectives:

Focus on your strengths

Develop clarity on the strengths you want to use in your work. This will guide which collaborations you get involved in, what you say no to, and what you teach others to solve for.

For Darren, an HR executive at a global tech company, his clear strength is solving thorny problems through a network approach. "I know I'm one of those people who love to run at things that are complex and hard," he told me. "I love looking at complex problems that most people would run away from. I love pulling those problems apart into micro-pieces and solving them incrementally by going to the network to find folks who are going to help me unpack the problem and solve it."

However, with many years' experience, he's also a whiz at handling the routine decisions that come up all the time in HR. In fact, he recognizes that because he spends so much of his time dealing with super-complicated issues—"problems with long, long tails"—it can be tempting to take a break from these headaches by focusing on quick, easy, low-level decisions.

"When I'm having a bad day where I'm working on something hard and thorny, and I know it's going to take me three months to get it done, the most seductive thing for me is to get an email with a question that I know the answer to or with a request for a decision that I can easily make," Darren said. "It's seductive because I know I can type in the answer, hit the 'send' button, and feel that I've accomplished something that helped someone. I know I would feel, 'Damn, I got something done today!' It's like when I pull weeds in the yard on the weekend: I can look back in a couple of hours and say I actually did something tangible!"

But his superpower of being able to quickly dispatch low-level decisions is a strength he doesn't want to deploy. He restrains himself from using it. "I know that if I dealt with those problems, I'd just be stroking my personal ego rather than doing what's best," he said. "I know that what the company needs me to do, and what I need to do for my team's growth, is to hand off these requests to people on my team. Their job is to learn, and this is how they learn, so if I dealt with a request myself, I'd be taking away their ability to do their job. So instead of giving in to the temptation to deal with these issues myself, I'll say to a team member, 'Here's something that could be kind of interesting. Go work it out. I trust you.'"

This self-discipline helps him stay aligned with the values he wants to live and the identity he wants to build his life around. He is able to continue to develop his team and grow into the kind of visionary and inspiring executive he wants to be. He knows he can't stay focused on the big picture if he lets himself get absorbed in collaborations that should be other people's responsibilities.

Like Darren, the most-efficient collaborators have figured out how to build their important aspirations into their work and their lives.

Focus on connections

Proactively initiate network connections important to professional and personal success. Too often we completely overlook the fact that we are social beings who function within networks of social beings. In the hundreds of interviews I conducted, it was vanishingly rare for these accomplished individuals to even acknowledge that their ideas and achievements had anything to do with other people's contributions. This is just human nature. Most of the time we put ourselves at the center of our success and forget about the impact of the networks around us.

Yet research shows that we are all guided by our connections to others. We shouldn't forget that fact. We should actively seek out and make connections with people who can help us meet our goals, and in so doing create powerful networks that I describe as *noninsular*.

A noninsular network is one that takes you off your island, whatever that island is ("insular" comes from the Latin word for island).

By spanning boundaries, noninsular networks offer rich opportunities to get help with projects, tap into ideas, and gain a broad perspective. Efficient collaborators initiate these connections across short, medium, and long time horizons and do not let the more-distant-horizon interactions fall away, as so often happens to people who are collaboratively overwhelmed (more on this in chapter 6).

Block time in your calendar for more-reflective work

Acutely aware that time is their most important asset, the most-efficient collaborators use their calendars as tools to avoid unnecessary collaborations and consistently move toward their North Star objectives through their professional and personal activities. They'll typically build rolling calendars and create categories that are important to their overall success and make sure there are activities in each of these categories in each of the time periods.

Many specifically make sure they include enough energizing interactions sprinkled throughout any given week to offset the less-energizing interactions. Scheduling energizing interactions allows you to maintain your sense of purpose and engagement so you can consistently be present for people and build supportive networks. (See the Coaching Break, "Strategic Calendaring.")

Manage to your best rhythm of work

What rhythm of work has proved to be most effective for you? If early morning is a time of energy and clarity, what's your best use of that time? Maybe it's engaging in creative thought.

Late afternoon is a desert for many of us, a time when we seek out the oases of small workrooms equipped with comfortable chairs so we can close our eyes for a few minutes. But for others, late afternoon is a low-pressure time of relaxed clarity—perfect for knocking out emails or organizing next week's calendar. Some people gain new energy late at night after everyone else has gone to bed, becoming intensely creative in the final hours of the day.

Strategic Calendaring

The best way to manage your time is to create a visual model of it. That's why strategic calendaring is so important. Follow these steps:

1. **Define your priorities.** That always comes first. Don't let your priorities be defined by others or by societal expectations that you will attain lofty positions that may not line up with what you want to do or be. Be clear on capabilities you want to distinguish yourself on and develop in the coming five years and values you want to experience in your career.

2. **Create a development plan for yourself and then reach out to a network of advisers.** Don't focus exclusively on people who fulfill the roles you want; instead, include people who live the way you most want to live, whether they are older or younger and whether they are inside or outside of your traditional career path.

3. **Create a weekly, biweekly, or monthly rolling calendar.** Base the calendar on holistic categories that are important to your overall success. Categories might include current business contributions, strategic or long-term planning, team and network development, personal or professional development, and mental and physical well-being.

4. **Set aside a one-hour block at the end or beginning of each time period.** Use the time to create your calendar for the next period.

5. **Incorporate your priorities into the calendar.** Set up meetings with people to focus on what you want to do. At the same time, your priorities should guide your decisions about which meetings you *don't* need to attend. Some people color-code their calendars to help them see the big picture. For example, label meetings that you must attend as green, those that you don't need to attend as red.

(continued)

6. **Use your calendar to limit the time that you allocate to work, email, or social media.** Create buffering strategies such as rules around when you will answer email, check instant messaging or phone messages, and leave work.

7. **Lock in important activities related to your objectives.** Shape your planned interactions to create new possibilities and generate work that you find engaging.

8. **Adhere to your calendar to fulfill commitments.** Those commitments include family, exercise, or community involvement.

9. **Make sure that your interactions are balanced for maximum energy.** If you know you're going to have to go through a de-energizing interaction, balance it with an energizing interaction so that you can restore your sense of purpose in your work.

10. **Employ buffering mechanisms such as administrative assistants.** Allow teams to have visibility into blocks of time they can schedule with you in relation to key activities, deliverables, and important milestones, but otherwise limit people's access to you.

Listen to your rhythms. Work with them; manage to them. Schedule the most important activities to match your expected surges of energy and creativity, and reserve the most routine stuff for your dead times.

As he gained an understanding of essential collaboration, Scott became highly attuned to his rhythm of work and began sticking to it. For years, he had been in the habit of starting on email first thing in the morning (I got some messages from him as early as 3 a.m.). The idea was to get the emails out of the way so he didn't hold people up and he could get on to his strategic work. But, of course, that never happened. Email begets email.

He realized that "by answering emails, I was letting other people start my day for me," he said. So, he reversed the order of his activities, using the early-morning time for what mattered most to him. "I learned that I was much better off starting with the reflective, creative work. I forced myself *not* to look at email. Then I had my EA block time for email through the day to take care of urgent items. As people got used to this pattern, they quit sending me emails on big issues that should have been discussions anyway." (See the Coaching Break, "Taking Small Steps.")

Sculpt your work to align with your objectives

If we're not careful, we can get pulled into all sorts of collaborative work that has nothing to do with where we want to go in our careers or who we want to be. For example, Tristan, a manager at a consulting firm that partners with state governments to build wireless networks, was good at making social connections. He had a reputation as someone who would say yes to just about anything: *yes* was his answer to colleagues who needed assistance finding sites for wireless nodes; *yes* was his answer to wrangling permits; *yes* to helping debug a piece of proprietary software; *yes* to giving talks at schools about the smart grid.

He said yes for many reasons, chief among them that he enjoyed interesting, challenging projects. He had a big appetite for life, and his firm allowed him to eat his fill. The CEO appreciated the way Tristan spread his enthusiasm from one corner of the company to the other, so she encouraged him to cross boundaries.

But because Tristan's efforts lacked the purpose and thoughtfulness that characterize the most-efficient collaborators, he had never been able to set a clear direction for his career. He did a lot of this and a lot of that but ended up going in circles. Finally, feeling frustrated, he clarified his North Star objectives: he wanted to sculpt his career by building on his interest in and skill at managing operations, and he was determined to help the company grow beyond its current regional presence. In addition to using strategic calendaring and finding alternative go-to people who could handle the kinds of requests he was used to handling himself, Tristan went a step further,

Taking Small Steps

Contrary to what most people assume, shifting routine work to others doesn't require a massive effort. Instead, it's a matter of a few small steps.

- **Develop an awareness of others' expertise and aspirations.** Knowing where expertise lies in the network broadens the way you conceptualize problems and solutions. Knowing others' aspirations informs how you enroll people and diffuse owner- ship. Every week, meet with colleagues and/or employees or use social-media tools to extend your understanding of others' knowledge and motivations.

- **Set expectations.** If you're a leader, establish expectations that people around you will solve problems collaboratively rather than come to you for approval or face time. Look for opportuni- ties to distribute work within your networks in ways that might prevent excessive collaborative demands from coming to you. For example, pairing high and low performers can leverage the team's expertise and provide developmental support to lower performers. Every week, find a way to provide informal recogni- tion for others' collaborative problem solving.

- **Engage others in co-creation of solutions early.** They should feel ownership and begin building collaborative relationships that help you step out of tasks. One leader's steadfast rule is *I never do anything alone.* This stands in contrast to less-effective people who think they should hold on to an idea until it has developed and then have to invest time and effort to get others up to speed and con- nected to the right people in the network. Every week, bring some- one with you to meetings, client interactions, or lunches as a way to engage others early and diffuse ownership of work and innovation.

getting involved in operational aspects of the firm that he had previously stayed out of.

Not only did he become more effective overall, he also got the attention of the CEO as an operational maven. When the COO position opened up, he got the job.

Shaping Role Interdependencies

The second set of structural practices focus on roles and the interdependencies among them—in other words, these practices are about being mindful and proactive about who depends on whom, for what, and to what extent.

Sometimes we inadvertently invite people to become too dependent on us. An extreme example is Asher, who is part of a team that handles back-office functions for a global consulting firm. Asher's team members are known for their collegiality. But if you spend any time in his area, you'll see that it's not just collegiality that constantly brings his coworkers to his cube. Asher has a reputation for knowing how all the intranet applications work. Sometimes a line forms at his desk. "Asher, when you get done helping that person with the KM app, could you help me with the scheduling process?"

Asher spends hours every week helping his coworkers on technical-support issues, even when he knows he shouldn't. For example, when the company rolled out its brand-new expense system, he was the only person who seemed to be able to figure it out. It became a perfect storm: a very-user-unfriendly system plus a very-user-friendly colleague. So, he answered all comers who needed help, leaving him with hardly any time for his own work. Now he doesn't know how to get out of the situation. He is a prototypical example of how easily servant-minded people can get stuck under a burden of collaboration overload.

In addition to being inundated with requests from his coworkers, Asher continues to get a steady stream of assignments from above, and rarely do these requesters ask what else he's working on or whether he has the bandwidth to take on something new. But like most of us, he doesn't want to hesitate and doesn't want to be a complainer. So, he feels that he has no choice but to say yes.

"Shaping role interdependencies" means using role management as a buffer. Erecting barriers between you and sources of overload by understanding and managing the network will help you systematically buy back time. The most adept collaborators use the following practices.

Periodically review calendars and email

Do this to define information requests that you are involved in and that could be either reallocated to less-overloaded people or more efficiently addressed with a revised process or policy.

We saw Scott do this well. He defined information requests, routine decisions, and meetings that could be removed from his work stream. Do as Scott did, reviewing your email and calendar on a continuing basis. Look at the past, look at the future: What are you doing, against your better judgment? Are all of those collaborations necessary, not only for you, but for the organization?

Categorize requests into action requests and informational requests. Which of those actions are really required? Which of those requests could be answered by someone else? Do the same for decisions and meetings. Could you reduce your collaboration load by 10 percent? 20 percent? More? This is the beginning of creating a buffer. (See the Coaching Break, "Rethinking Routines.")

Proactively shape others' expectations of your role

This may sound like the practice of sculpting your work, which was discussed earlier, but it's different. This is about shaping expectations. Across all industries, top performers are well aware that a request from a colleague or leader can suddenly launch a vast amount of collaborative churn.

Top collaborators rarely view requests as locked-in work that they or their teams must accomplish. Instead, they clarify and shape ex-

Rethinking Routines

With a little effort, you should be able to identify a number of opportunities to let go of routine activities. Look back four months in your calendar and your email, and two months ahead in your schedule. Scan through each day and follow these steps:

1. **Notice** calendar items and email subject lines that indicate recurring or routine informational requests or times when people seek you out for expertise in areas that are no longer central to your success.

2. **Reflect** carefully on the nature of decisions you get pulled into. Routine decisions often become embedded in organizations because the knee-jerk reaction to an issue or crisis was to create a policy, process, or procedure that now consumes an enormous amount of collaborative time.

3. **Identify** four to five opportunities to shift processes or nominate alternative go-to people to reduce the collaborative time burden.

4. **Bring in a coach**, team member, or significant other if you're having trouble identifying opportunities to let go of routine activities. Often, we become blind to these opportunities.

pectations to give themselves or their teams greater space to function effectively, on reasonable time scales, and to apply their best capabilities. The challenge is to shift your mindset from seeing work as a list of responsibilities imposed by others, with no input from you, and begin proactively understanding and shaping the expectations around the requests coming to you.

First, identify who is driving your work, or your team's work. Maybe it's just your boss, but there may be other constituencies involved, such as customers or other kinds of stakeholders. Then, where possible, set up meetings with these individuals or with representatives of these groups. Discuss their objectives and their understanding of their problems.

Clarity will help, especially when you're dealing with requests that come down through a faceless chain of command. One manufacturing leader described a scenario in which a big and urgent request came from a senior vice president's chief of staff. She had the presence of mind to ask the SVP to clarify the ask and found that the true need "was actually a much smaller request. The chief of staff either didn't get quite as much info as I did or didn't provide me with the context the SVP provided about what it might be used for."

Another manager, a consumer-products leader, has learned to always ask questions about the ultimate use and desired impact of the work her team is being asked to do. For example, her CEO made a sweeping decree that for the company's foray into the India market, it would need a set of new, locally focused brands. Foreseeing extensive churn in the form of design efforts and management structures, the manager asked the CEO how much would really be gained—would it be worth the effort? He was annoyed at first, but he assigned someone to quantify the potential advantage of localized but unfamiliar brands over foreign but familiar brands. The estimate showed there would be little advantage, so the initiative was scrapped.

"Probing in this way for a minute or two sometimes might catch the leader off guard or be a little frustrating at first," the manager said. "But over the years, I have probably saved ten person-years of unnecessary work by reframing what my teams deliver, and in what time frame, through a couple of probing questions. But you have to catch this in that small window when they are asking."

If you're a leader, be transparent about your—or your team's—goals, capabilities, and interests. At the same time, be forthright about the volume of demands you are already facing. Often, leaders and other stakeholders make requests without understanding the time demands of the work. If you are a team leader meeting demands from multiple stakeholders, put the names of the stakeholders on a whiteboard; then, in columns under each one, write the initiatives you are working on for that person or group, in the order of prioritization that you feel is appropriate. Describe the threshold level of initiatives your team can support.

Now that your stakeholders know your or your team's goals, capabilities, interests, and workload, ask them to clarify their priorities in light of these factors. Urge them to discuss their true needs. Look for opportunities to reframe their requests so that you can simultaneously meet the needs of two or more parties. A face-to-face or virtual meeting is the preferred way to create this kind of alignment, but if you do not have that luxury, simple polling technologies can be effective.

Come to a collective agreement on work that is most critical to accomplish and that falls within your aims, capabilities, and interests or those of your team. Talk about alternative ways you—or, if you are a team leader, your team—could deliver results. Discuss how you could provide an outcome of even greater value than you are providing now.

Position your involvement in collaborative work to ensure you add unique value

This means finding tasks, projects, and initiatives where you and you alone can have a significant impact because of your abilities and interests. Audrey, a manager at a women's clothing retailer, had become exasperated that customers weren't responding well to her company's efforts to build a strong online presence. Audrey's job was to manage a number of physical stores in the Southeast, but previously she had spent a year in a graduate marketing program. Though academia was not for her and she never did get her PhD, she had learned quite a bit from a leading researcher in the area of online customer-relationship management. Now she could see that her company was failing to grasp a basic reality of CRM, that customers want their clothing retailers to meet their emotional needs, such as to be listened to and treated with respect.

Much as she loved managing stores—working with salespeople, talking with customers—she saw that she had a unique contribution to make, so she began writing to a marketing executive she knew, offering her insights. It took a while for the company to recognize the value of Audrey's insights, but she eventually did get placed on the online-CRM team. This was a prime example of an individual positioning her involvement in collaborative work where she was able to add unique value.

Address one-off requests all at once

Sometimes one-off requests demand immediate responses, but often they don't, in which case you can aggregate and address them all at once in regularly scheduled standing meetings. These meetings provide opportunities for team members to learn to turn to each other for help, rather than always seeking out the leader. Agendas should encourage participants to develop awareness of one another's work and skills. Standing meetings can also promote collaborative efficiency by reducing or streamlining excessive one-off requests or disruptions.

It's important not to let such meetings go off track. If you schedule a standing meeting—every two weeks, say—make sure that people speak only if they have real issues to discuss, and that if all issues are settled, the meeting ends early. Don't meet simply to meet or talk simply to talk. Stay focused on productive use of time and promoting more-efficient collaborations.

I realize that after all the discussion of cutting out unnecessary meetings, I may sound as though I'm contradicting myself by advocating standing meetings, but what's great about them is that after a while, you can begin to have people post issues ahead of time that they plan to raise in the standing meetings. They can post these issues to a shared space that the relevant group can see. Over time, encourage team members to collaborate directly with each other to solve problems. What many leaders find is that the week leading up to the meeting might start with ten items and end with most, if not all, solved because the team is also developing a capability for resolution. If all the issues have been resolved, you can decide to not hold the meeting, or use it for interactions that might reenergize the group.

. . .

Finding and staying true to your North Star aspirations is key to whether you get overrun by collaborative demands or chart your own path. Put another way, it is key to whether you play defense or offense.

Playing defense means taking an ad hoc approach to dealing with requests for help. You end up letting network interactions and collaborative demands define you. You get caught up in politics as you constantly try to appease people. "Playing defense sucks," one leader said. "You are always reactive and living in fear. The only way to get out of it is to get clarity on who you are and what you want to do and start forging a path that enables you to get there."

So far, we've looked at beliefs and structure as aids in helping you play offense and save yourself from collaboration overload. But on the path to essential collaboration, there's one additional thing more-efficient collaborators do—they streamline collaborative practices. I will discuss this in the next chapter.

THE TAKEAWAY FOR YOU

Imposing Structure That Can Help You Avoid Overload

We've looked at numerous structural approaches to relieving collaboration overload, but which ones matter to *you*? I've taken all the practices we've discussed in this chapter and recast them in the form of "I" statements so you can picture applying them to yourself. Imagine adopting these practices, and check the box for the one or two that you think could be most helpful in your current situation. Then ask someone who knows you well to do the same, with your tendencies in mind—what solutions does that person see as potentially having the biggest impact on you?

STRUCTURAL PRACTICES: I have clarity on the strengths I want to employ in my work, the values I want to live through my career, and the identity I want to build my life around. This clarity guides which collaborations I get involved in, what I say no to, and what I teach others to solve without me.

☐ You

☐ Someone who knows you well

Solutions you could adopt from the most-efficient collaborators

In order to engage in collaborative work in a way that will be more meaningful to you, be clear about strengths you want to deploy, values you want to live through your career, and personal aspirations that you want to build into your life. To do this, develop clarity on your North Star objectives, focusing on what you truly care about—not society's definition of success as a certain role or promotion or way of spending your time. Maintain outside commitments to family, exercise, or community involvement that can pull you into different domains and serve as buffers to work.

STRUCTURAL PRACTICES: I proactively initiate network connections important to my professional and personal success.

☐ You

☐ Someone who knows you well

Solutions you could adopt from the most-efficient collaborators

Rather than play defense and let collaborative demands define you, play offense by being proactive in network development, focusing on spheres you should invest in for depth or complementary expertise. Start with people you know for introductions or reach out to those you don't know with a request to explore overlaps and complementarities. Then follow up on those leads. End meetings by asking: Who else should I be speaking with, and can you connect me?

By doing this, you can build rich, noninsular networks through external connections and boundary-spanning collaborations within your organization. These connections will help you see the world differently and give you a sense of influence and power that enables you to take courageous action in saying no to collaborative requests.

STRUCTURAL PRACTICES: I block time in my calendar for more-reflective work.

☐ You
☐ Someone who knows you well

Solutions you could adopt from the most-efficient collaborators

Impose structure through your calendar to ensure that activities you get involved with—both professional and personal—pull you to your North Star objectives. Structure activities through the week with an eye to personal motivation and enthusiasm, alternating energizing with less-energizing interactions to help manage your sense of purpose and engagement.

Define priorities to guide calendar decisions and be very clear on which meetings you need to attend and which you don't need to attend.

STRUCTURAL PRACTICES: I manage to my best rhythm of work.

☐ You
☐ Someone who knows you well

Solutions you could adopt from the most-efficient collaborators

Listen to your own rhythms. Instead of fighting with them, work with them and manage to them. Look at your daily and weekly patterns: Where are the crunch points and the reflection times, and how well do they match your surges of energy and creativity? Rearrange your schedule so you can apply your greatest vitality to the most important activities and reserve the most routine work for your least-productive times.

STRUCTURAL PRACTICES: I sculpt my work to align with my North Star objectives.

☐ You
☐ Someone who knows you well

Solutions you could adopt from the most-efficient collaborators

Shape the work to match your capabilities, interests, and goals—or, if you're a leader, those of your team. Engage in conversations with team members to find out about their goals and aspirations.

Align the work with what you or your team members can do best and are most motivated to do. Use one-on-one meetings to create semiannual development goals for each team member and then craft each person's work around their goals.

STRUCTURAL PRACTICES: I periodically review my calendar and email to define information requests that I am involved in and that could be reallocated to less-overloaded people, posted to a website, or more efficiently addressed with a revised process or policy.

☐ You
☐ Someone who knows you well

Solutions you could adopt from the most-efficient collaborators

Periodically reflecting on demands and shifting those that you do not add value to—or that do not add value to you—is critical to collaborative efficiency over time. Look through your calendar for routine or recurring activities that you can shift to others as developmental opportunities—or those that can be halted altogether or made far more efficient by altering a process or decision threshold.

Reflect carefully on the nature of decisions you are getting pulled into. Identify four to five opportunities to shift processes or nominate alternative people on routine decisions.

STRUCTURAL PRACTICES: I proactively shape others' expectations of my role.

☐ You
☐ Someone who knows you well

Solutions you could adopt from the most-efficient collaborators

This may sound similar to "I sculpt my work to align with my North Star objectives," above, but it's not about shaping work, it's about shaping expectations. If you know it's going to take you a while to meet a leader's request, proactively manage what is expected of you. Be transparent on what your level of engagement in issues and discussions will be and clarify that a nonresponse from you doesn't signal disengagement or lack of appreciation.

Set up meetings to clarify response times needed and prioritization guidelines. Demonstrate that you want people to solve problems collaboratively around you rather than come to you for approval or face time. Use informal recognition in meetings and group communications to celebrate this kind of problem solving. Look for opportunities to distribute collaborations in the network in a way that might stop demands from coming to you.

STRUCTURAL PRACTICES: I position my involvement in collaborative work where I add unique value.

☐ You
☐ Someone who knows you well

Solutions you could adopt from the most-efficient collaborators

Think of the work and network simultaneously. Invest time to become aware of expertise in your network so that you can broaden the way you conceptualize solutions. Envision projects as activities you map onto people in your network. Enroll people in activities by knowing their aspirations. Step out of the way, or engage only where you have unique value to contribute.

Engage others in co-creation of solutions early so that they can begin building collaborative relationships that help you step out of the middle of the work.

STRUCTURAL PRACTICES: I address one-off requests all at once.

- ☐ You
- ☐ Someone who knows you well

Solutions you could adopt from the most-efficient collaborators

Standing meetings can promote collaborative efficiency by reducing or streamlining excessive one-off requests or disruptions. Schedule periodic meetings that fit the rhythm of work. Structure meetings so that the opening is focused on priorities and directional issues that ensure alignment of the team around core goals and objectives. Remind people of the "why." Conclude by having team members share one succinct win and one succinct challenge.

Employ a collaborative tool for the team to post issues and challenges to cover in the standing meeting. Then use meeting time to focus on what needs to be discussed—not update information that people can read.

5

Alter Behaviors to Streamline Collaboration Practices

Reina woke up feeling energized about her day. She was an account manager at a pharmaceutical marketing firm, and her newest account was about to introduce a medication for depression. She had already received a text from the drug company's marketing chief with ideas for the 9 a.m. kickoff meeting. She scrolled down; it was a long text, too long for her to absorb right now as she was getting out of bed, but she understood and shared his excitement. The drug had been in the pipeline for years, and everyone was thrilled that it was finally hitting the market.

There was the usual chaos at breakfast, but her husband volunteered to braid the girls' hair, so Reina was able to get out of the house on time, for once. During her commute, she took a call about coverage for two upcoming maternity leaves in her creative department. A successful resolution to that issue left her feeling she had accomplished something before she even got to the office—a great start to the day.

Her assistant was already in and hard at work, making sure that everyone who had been invited to the kickoff planned to attend. Arriving at her desk, Reina glanced at the boldface subject lines that filled her inbox. There were a lot of messages, but they could wait. She spent the hour she had before the kickoff getting ready for it. When she walked into the meeting at 9 a.m., it was exactly as she had envisioned: *everyone* was there in the big conference room.

The chairs around the oval table were filling up, so it was good that her assistant had put extra rows along the windows and walls. Reina overheard someone asking someone else what the meeting was about: "Why are we here?"

She ignored that and positioned herself near the screen at the head, making sure the tech person had set up all the AV connections. Platters of pastries and fruit had been set out, and people were helping themselves.

"Is there an agenda?" someone asked her.

"Not necessary," she replied. "We're just going to talk about the launch and hear from a few people. We'll let it happen organically."

She waited for things to quiet down; by then, it was an overflow crowd, with people standing in the doorways. Reina started, "This is a big day for all of us." She talked a bit about the new drug and said they'd be hearing from leaders of the pharma company via video link.

A few hands went up. Could she recap what the drug does and how it's different? Could she summarize the marketing plan? She promised that the questions would be answered as the meeting unfolded. She introduced the drug company CEO, who talked about his hopes for the new product. He introduced his marketing VP, who discussed the marketing plan. (Reina realized that she had never found time to read the lengthy email that the VP had sent her early that morning, but no matter.) The chief medical officer talked about the drug's mechanism, and there was a promotional video.

Time passed. The meeting started to drag. A few people drifted out. At the top of the hour, there was a sudden collective movement for the door, like at the end of a high school class. People were eager to go. The video link was shut down, and people grabbed the last pastries.

"You've got another meeting downstairs," Reina's assistant said. "Right now." So, it was off to the next one, where Reina sat to the side and started to look at her emails. She paid no attention to what was going on in the meeting, but that was no loss, because she didn't really have to be there anyway. She was just there to "show the marketing flag," as she often said.

She counted thirty-three unread messages in her inbox. She also saw five texts that she had to deal with. She knew it would go on like that all day. The energy she had felt during her commute was quickly slipping away. This was a familiar sensation—by midmorning, she often felt she had lost control of her day. She knew she would never catch up before going home. And then there would be requests from her husband, calls from her mother about her bad back, and calls from her sister asking for help with something or other. She would inevitably be up half the night dealing with work stuff. How did this happen?

The Root Problem

Reina's situation probably feels familiar to you. More often than is healthy, we all live this way, dealing with a huge volume and vast diversity of demands that come to us via professional and personal relationships.

It's tempting to look for easy answers to overload by obsessing over big inefficiencies that are out of our control, such as demands from unpredictable bosses. But usually the way out is by focusing instead on the small items we can influence and not allowing them to creep around us too much. It's about avoiding the death of a thousand cuts. Figure out what you have control over, what you can influence. Then play offense on these items.

Huge efficiencies are found by implementing better norms of practice around how we use the range of collaborative tools at our disposal. Let's say that Reina employed a best practice of scheduling her meetings for forty-five minutes each instead of an hour. Let's say she imposed more order through agendas and had someone capture and post meeting notes, eliminating maybe twenty texts throughout the day from people looking for clarity. And let's say she agreed with her team on a few simple norms on email length and use that had the effect of removing twenty emails and making another sixty of them more efficient to read and respond to.

All small stuff, right? And—as the cynical will note—this is not solving meetings or email in the aggregate. You may be saying, "I want a solution for the whole problem!"

All too often, in pursuit of a neat, elegant solution for the whole problem, people give up trying to make things marginally better. They won't take steps to streamline 60 emails with direct reports because that solution wouldn't work for the other 120 emails coming from bosses, clients, and stakeholders. But usually there is no elegant solution to the whole problem. Playing offense against overload is more like a brawl than a ballet. The winners are the ones who relentlessly claw time back through many small actions.

If Reina shortened those five meetings by a quarter-hour each, she'd get back seventy-five minutes in that one day. By eliminating the twenty texts, she'd get back maybe twenty minutes, figuring a minute each (and that doesn't include the time it takes to get back on task, which I will come to in a moment). Removing twenty emails would give her another twenty minutes, and streamlining sixty emails would give her maybe thirty additional minutes. Overall, she could claw back 145 minutes in one day alone.

But let's go deeper. *Channel inefficiency*—misuse of meetings, email, text, phone calls, and the like—is really a surface issue. Yes, it's real and it hurts us every day. But what's going on underneath is the more pressing problem: we're failing to create efficient interaction norms. We're not enabling cultures of efficient collaboration in our organizations.

And this is, at root, a *behavior* problem. Our own behavior creates unhealthy norms around the way we interact and generates the conditions for overload. Because it's a behavior problem, we can change it, but we have to be proactive and engage others.

Most time-management books treat each of us in isolation and tell us how to get faster and more organized. But getting faster and more efficient often means that demands will come back to us faster. Email begets email. Being super organized and execution oriented can create overreliance on us as teams push us into the hero role.

Preventing overload through death by a thousand cuts is a two-step process. First, you create channel efficiency, but then, crucially, you attack the underlying norms that create inefficient communication.

I will discuss best practices for each step. Some of those will be called out in detail in the "Coaching Break" sidebars.

The Meetings Channel

Most managers' calendars are like Reina's, filled with meetings from the beginning to the end of each day. But it's not just the number of meetings that bogs people down. It's the way the meetings are initiated, organized, and conducted.

Focus on desired outcomes, include only those necessary, and ensure meetings are efficient

Reina provides good examples of what *not* to do. It's a red flag if attendees ask questions like "What is this meeting about?" or "Why are we here?" or "Is there an agenda?" Reina never stated the meeting's purpose, nor did she send out preliminary information to help attendees get up to speed on the new drug.

Reina's comment that the meeting would unfold "organically" is another red flag. There can be times, such as early in projects, when this approach works. But unstructured meetings happen too often and, because they don't have an explicit purpose or clear agenda, attendees quickly become disengaged. This is a classic misuse of collaborative time. Then Reina allowed her own time to be misused by participating in a meeting that she had no real need to attend, and she misused that meeting by sitting there tending to her email.

See the Coaching Break, "Efficient Meetings" for strategies that the most-efficient collaborators described as a series of healthy norms that help them realize efficiencies *before* a meeting, *during* a meeting, and *after* a meeting. Before a meeting, they ask themselves, What do I need, and why? Am I clear on what I want to accomplish in this meeting?

Efficient Meetings

Meetings are the channel of choice for an array of collaborative decision-making, problem-solving, and innovation activities. Research shows that when meetings follow an appropriate degree of organization and process for the task at hand, work output and efficiency greatly improve. There are numerous ways to provide such organization. They can be broken down into *pre-meeting*, *meeting*, and *post-meeting* strategies.

Pre-Meeting

- Stay focused by asking yourself: What do I need, and why? Am I clear on what I want to accomplish in this meeting?

- State the meeting's purpose and spell out objectives or expectations for outcomes.

- Publish the agenda, the timeline, the attendee list, and expectations for how and when people will contribute, and for how long. This includes specifying facilitative roles: Who will make presentations? Who will manage discussions of subtopics? Place these and any other informational materials into an online team space.

- Keep meetings as small as possible (when the number of participants grows beyond a manageable size, assign team leads or liaisons to smaller groups, using shared team spaces to exchange information whenever possible).

- Touch base with people who are tangentially involved but don't actually need to be there and reassure them that it's OK if they don't show up.

- Send out preliminary information so that meeting time is spent on the best use of attendees' expertise and expect attendees to actually read this preparatory material.

Meeting

- If you are using videoconferencing, encourage people to show up early while previous videoconferences are ending, so that there is overlap and people can bump into one another, just as they might in the hallway in person or if they poked their heads into others' cubes (this facilitates informal interactions that make remote workers feel more integrated into day-to-day interactions).

- Follow the agenda and objectives.

- Don't waste time at the beginning of the meeting to catch up those who missed the last one.

- Require people to be fully present (not answering emails or texts) and contributing concisely or, if they agree with what has been said, not contributing at all (rather than contributing purely for status or visibility).

- If it's a videoconference, require people to keep their cameras on at all times, even when screen sharing (the ability to see body language and gestures strengthens the interactions and fosters relationship building).

- Adhere to process guidelines to stay on task within rough time-lines; yet, at the same time, keep enough slack in the agenda to allow for informal interactions (this enriches relationships, as people find points of communality).

- Establish norms of how and when to disagree; these norms should include no sidebar disagreements during the meeting.

- Keep meetings brief, and don't slavishly adhere to the allotted time; don't let a meeting expand to fill the prescribed slot.

(continued)

- End five minutes early, don't run late, and don't convey important information as people are leaving. Many organizations use agile methods such as holding meetings in stairways or other common spaces, limiting meetings to twenty minutes, banning food, and asking people to stand up (if able) for the duration.

Post-Meeting

- Send follow-up emails on agreements, commitments, and next steps.

- Reinforce a norm that people who miss the meeting own catching up and coming to the next one informed about what they missed.

Then they state the meeting's purpose, posting the agenda, establishing expectations for how and when people will contribute, and sending out preliminary material. During the meeting, they follow the agenda and require people to contribute appropriately, given the objectives. Afterward, they send follow-up emails on next steps.

Although Reina saw her kickoff meeting as a big success, her poor process ended up wasting people's time and deprived the core team of a chance to discuss substantive issues and challenges that lay ahead.

The Email Channel

While Reina was catching up on emails in her 10 a.m. meeting, she clicked a message with the subject line "A few things to go over . . . Please read!!!" It was from a person working on one of the firm's oldest accounts, a pharma company struggling to revitalize its image. It began with "I know you're busy, but you asked me to spell out the issues with this client in an email, so here it is—PLEASE RESPOND ASAP, as I have to get back to them!!!"

This particular individual was always taking this kind of tone with her. Reina briefly wondered why she tolerated it, but she put that thought aside and dug in, trying to get through the email quickly. She knew that if she didn't deal with this, the sender would be on her back all day, calling her and sending follow-up emails.

There was a long analysis of the current issues. Reina was making progress in understanding the problem when she got a text on her phone from another person asking if she had looked at his email about a plan for a different client's campaign. It was very urgent, he said.

Reina had to switch gears to think about this. A new campaign . . . Ah, yes, she knew what it was about: the new campaign was targeted to physicians, and in fact it had been Reina's idea, something she was really excited about. But why was it "very urgent"? The text didn't say, so she went back to her inbox and looked for an email from that person. She found it, opened it, scanned it, and closed it. The matter wasn't that urgent after all.

She put it aside, but then for a moment she couldn't remember what she had been thinking about before. Her brain felt addled. She would often start on a task, then get interrupted by something and have trouble resuming it. In darker moments, she worried about this and wondered if the stress was getting to her, if she was getting old, or if there was something wrong with her brain.

A Brief Interruption . . . about Interruptions

Researchers who study thinking would say there's nothing wrong with Reina's brain. What happens to her happens to everyone. When you're working on a complex task, you create mental structures such as images and categories to help you understand the problem. These "schemas" are fleeting, as though written in smoke. If you're interrupted, they hang in the air of your mind for a while, but not for long. If the interruption is too protracted, when you go back to them, they've drifted away.

The schemas that Reina had begun creating as she tried to solve the problem-client issue had dissolved during the interruption. Afterward, it was a struggle to recreate them and resume where she had left off.

Email is a particularly insidious platform for interruption, because of its omnipresence. The potential for disruption never goes away. But there are many additional channels of interruption: phone calls, texts, direct messages, pop-in requests, fire drills, news events, and so on. And the effect is the same—we get thrown off, and the switching costs mount up over the course of the day.

Interruption science has been going strong since it started in the 1800s in Europe with the beginnings of the study of cognition. Cognition researchers, unlike neuroscientists, don't focus on the physical hardware of the brain. Instead, they look at the software—at how thoughts and memories course through the mind.

The field took a big step forward in the 1950s with the work of American memory researchers Lloyd and Peggy Peterson. The Petersons, who raised four children together while teaching at Indiana University, helped develop a procedure still used in clinical research: they asked people to remember strings of letters, then interrupted them with tasks such as counting backward by threes, and then asked how many of the letters they could still recall.[1] The earlier memories got obliterated after as little as eighteen seconds of interruption.[2]

Research on interruptions has surged in the twenty-first century as a response to our always-on and always-interrupted digital culture. Within the past few years, two researchers in France analyzed the state of the art on the components of mental schemas, which they called "knowledge structures," and looked at what happens to them during interruptions. They reported that the literature demonstrates that "an interruption longer than 30 seconds would completely extinguish the components related to the primary task. Once the interruption is over, [the components of these schemas] must be reactivated completely in order to resume that task."[3]

And how long does it take, after an interruption, to get our bearings again and to piece together what we were working on before? Gloria Mark, a professor in informatics at UC Irvine, uses biosensors and ethnographic techniques to study the effects of disruption. She told one interviewer that after an interruption, "You have to completely shift your thinking . . . it takes an average of twenty-three minutes and fifteen seconds to get back to the task."[4] With practice, people do get better at adjusting to interruptions, but this adaptability comes at a cost, as she says in one of her research papers: people who were frequently interrupted "experienced a higher workload, more stress, higher frustration, more time pressure, and [greater] effort." This greater stress has negative consequences for health and performance.[5]

Let's say, conservatively, that of all the interruptions tormenting Reina during her day, three of them were avoidable. Let's also say that she lost the average recovery time of twenty-three minutes and fifteen seconds on each of those avoidable interruptions. That comes to one hour, nine minutes, and forty-five seconds lost. Add that to the 145 minutes of easily salvageable time that she wasted on meetings and inefficient communications, and you get three hours, thirty-four minutes, and forty-five seconds. In one day.

That's not *real* time, you might say. But isn't it? The loss of all these hours is exactly why we are exhausted at the end of the day. It's why we are doing email when we should be thinking strategically or spending time with family or friends. We all need to appreciate how truly damaging our constant disruptions, interruptions, and task switches can be over the long term so that we can begin to organize our behaviors in new ways.

Effective Use of Email

Email is in the top three presumed drivers of collaboration overload in every survey we have done. But the heart of the problem is not the technology itself but the culture of email use we all allow to persist.

The magic of efficient collaborators is that they recognize this and shape the collaboration norms in groups they can influence.

Adopt efficient norms of email

The employee who wielded the exclamation points and all caps succinctly summed up Reina's failure to establish efficient norms: "You asked me to spell out the issues with this client in an email." Reina routinely and explicitly asked people to use email as a means for hashing out the details of work, rather than as a tool to confirm expectations or set up times for face-to-face discussions.

Email is potentially a great tool. You can use it to reach out across units, hierarchical levels, geographies, and even organizational lines. But because of this power, it can quickly become a significant source of collaboration overload, disengagement, and performance degradation. The volume and diversity of messages create an enormous burden—invisible to all but the recipient. And because of the permanence of these communications, they consume us more than meetings or conversations as we think about and respond to issues.

The lack of physical cues in emails, or the kinds of subtleties that are expressed by voice, often leads to faulty assumptions about emails' tone, which can create additional work for everyone. The leanness becomes a particular problem if people try to use email to avoid in-person conflict; if there's disagreement, it may feel more comfortable to send an email, when a phone call or face-to-face meeting would be a faster and better way to deal with the problem. Email also follows us everywhere on our mobile devices. That means we often find ourselves responding late at night, early in the morning, or while we're on vacation.

The most-efficient collaborators were very clear about their behaviors around email. To reduce collaborative time, they establish guidelines for themselves and create healthy norms throughout their groups on how to use and deal with email. These guidelines fall into three categories—*format and organization of emails, use of email,* and *limiting email-related disruptions.* The guidelines include such best practices as establishing a maximum message length—the efficient collaborators don't waste time perfecting lengthy messages that others are forced to respond to (or don't read at all). Instead, they use outline structures with bullet points, create effective subject lines, and establish reasonable norms on response time. (See the Coaching Break, "Efficient Email.")

Reina didn't perceive the invisible and insidious effects of the unhealthy email norms she had tolerated and encouraged. She had gotten used to absorbing the inefficiencies and shrugging them off. She wasn't aware that eliminating just twenty daily emails and streamlining sixty more could result in time savings of nearly an hour in her busy workday. She didn't see that the behaviors that led to email inefficiencies were worth acting on—that she needed to learn how to change her behaviors so that she could minimize the inefficiencies.

You won't be surprised to hear that Reina's inefficient behaviors extended to her use of texting, instant messaging, and phone calls. In fact, she tended to blend channel inefficiencies together, as when she sat in meetings checking her phone for new emails and instant messages, and then reading and responding to them.

Direct Messaging and Rich Media

As with email, the norms that evolve around direct messaging and video have a big impact on the efficiency of our collaboration.

Use direct messaging to increase efficiency
of established relationships

Once relationships are established, direct messaging and direct-message platforms such as Slack can be effective as means for efficiently getting information to and from others in short, transactional exchanges. DMs also work well in informal communication or as a first point of contact. For example, send a direct message to inquire about availability, rather than calling cold.

Efficient Email

Email is the channel of choice for transactional exchanges such as distributing information or confirming agreements after a meeting. Healthy norms for email use fall into three categories—*format and organization of emails, use of email,* and *limiting email-related disruptions.*

Format and Organization

- Establish a maximum length. If you find yourself exceeding it, you need to communicate the idea via phone call, face-to-face meeting, or a well-thought-out written statement that the recipient can absorb when convenient.

- Move away from full-text paragraphs and instead use outline structures with bullet points.

- Clarify the "ask"—the objective of the email—in the first three sen tences; one leader in a global company said, "Give me the punch-line first." If that isn't possible, it's time to move to a richer channel.

- Use the subject line to convey the desired outcome—Is action required? Is it an FYI?—and the due date.

Usage

- Explicitly limit the volume of email. If you don't get alignment on a given topic after two emails, switch to a richer channel to help avoid churn and misunderstandings. Word your responses so as to discourage unnecessary follow-ups.

- Halt unnecessary cc'ing and "Reply to all." If you don't know how someone will use the information, consider taking that person off the thread.

- Use triage and filing practices such as color-coding cc or bcc emails so that you can review them appropriately; identify emails that require more than a minute's response and put them into an action folder for review later; establish rules to forward emails from specific senders to relevant people on the team; and use "out of office" or "not available" automatic notices to buy time when you need it.

- Celebrate email efficiency; call out channel uses that adhere to these norms.

- Remember that when you fire off emails early in the morning, late at night, or on the weekends, you send an unhealthy message to your team. If you must write emails during off-hours, use the delay feature to send them at the beginning of reasonable work hours so you don't create a stressful norm that everyone must be "always on."

- Create reasonable norms on response time. A cultural expectation that equates rapid response with working hard can send a group into a frenzy. Part of setting reasonable norms is establishing that in most circumstances, demanding that someone immediately read an email is an unacceptable imposition on their time.

Limiting Disruptions

- Establish a norm of setting aside specific times, such as 8 a.m. and 4 p.m. daily or three times a day, to read emails; turn off notifications at other times.

- Resist the temptation to constantly check for new email.

- Resist the impulse to read every new message right away.

- Establish norms around use of subject-line interrupters such as "Please read!!!" and "Urgent!!!"

However, DMs can easily become sources of interruptions and chaos. Don't start believing that you need to respond to all direct messages as rapidly as possible. Ignore them when you're in meetings or conversations. And don't let DM exchanges go on too long. If it takes longer than three or four texts, pick up the phone.

Support virtual collaborations with rich media and collaborative tools

Efficient collaborators know better than to over-rely on email when a video chat, phone call, or even a document-sharing application would provide fuller information and allow for greater nuance. They are quick to establish norms in their sphere of control that include things like: (1) consumable format norms (that is, length, bullet points, subject line to include action requested); (2) use of email only for informational purposes or when documenting/confirming agreements, not to resolve a conflict; (3) move to richer medium—phone or video call-–if disagreement lasts more than two emails; (4) leverage back-channel DM use to promote greater connectivity among team members; or (5) use Slack-oriented technology to create real-time experience and emphasize the emoticons and informal nature of discourse to recreate benefits of face-to-face interaction.

Although such technologies can impose significant collaborative costs if they're not used for the right purposes at the right time, they can yield tremendous benefits in enabling integration of expertise and capabilities by connecting people across geographic and organizational lines. More-efficient collaborators employ a broader range of collaborative tools and use them in the right way and at the right time to support collaborative work.

For example, efficient collaborators make excellent use of online spaces where teams can share information. These easily accessible repositories are great for documents such as project histories, lists of ongoing actions, financial data, surveys, participants' bios, and anticipated results. They allow everyone to see interconnection points and find shared interests and other commonalities. In some cases, teams create online "book of work" documents that list team mission and objectives, key priorities, and who is working on what aspect. Participants can open the document to see how their and others' work furthers the team's mission and objectives.

. . .

In order to understand the behaviors that drive interaction norms, we need to look at issues that may at first seem unconnected: generating a sense of purpose, teaching others to use our time well, and creating trust.

Create Efficient Interaction Norms

Let's go back to the story of Scott. You may recall that when things were at their worst, an average of 118 people in one unit came to him for information every day on matters large and small, a number that should have been much smaller. And 78 of these people said they couldn't meet their goals unless they got more of his time. As we saw, this situation and the overload it caused stemmed from Scott's own behaviors.

To his credit, Scott eventually came out of this phase of his life and grew into a true practitioner of essential collaboration, one of the people who helped me see what excellent collaboration really looks like. After he cleaned up his act and came to understand how to avoid overload, Scott was one of numerous people who showed me how they succeed not by pushing their ideas into situations or demanding help from people but rather by adhering to the following practices.

Draw people to collaborative work

There's a lot to think about when drawing people into collaborative work. One important reason why essential collaborators do this is that they understand their own limitations; they recognize that there is much they don't know. When he was overloaded, Scott, too, would sometimes recognize that he needed to tap others' expertise. But in those instances, he had to scramble to find the right people. Then he went to them cold, asking for their help.

These experts inevitably felt some resentment. They would pitch in, for sure—Scott could use the power of his personality or the authority of his position to enlist them—but chances are he would get only grudging compliance. He might even meet outright resistance.

Things are different now. Scott routinely identifies areas where his knowledge is insufficient, thinks carefully about people who could support his work, and seeks help from them. Rather than demanding involvement, he draws people in. He understands that he needs to create the time to give others status and recognize the work they do.

I saw this new approach in action. I noticed that Scott adopted a practice of giving first—he made an effort to forge connections with people and provide resources without expecting anything immediate in return. For example, without getting too involved himself, he helped a Canadian unit find experts within the US part of the company who could help solve a persistent IT problem. These connections became valuable later when he began working on an initiative to expand the company's Canadian presence. At one point, when he convened a working group to figure out how to manage payments for types of debit cards that were common in Canada but not in the United States, he started by asking basic questions: "Is this worth doing? Is it worth the time and effort?" Then he asked what aspects of the challenge people were most excited about. When group members expressed their views, he asked how he could best work with them. He singled out the quieter participants and made sure they were heard. Overall, it was a great example of envisioning and pursuing joint success.

Behaviors like these make the people around Scott feel excited about contributing time and effort. Today, if there is an emergency, Scott doesn't have to go to people cold and beg for—or demand—their help. The benefits can be felt throughout Scott's work. His employees and colleagues take inspired and motivated action on their own. They are more creative. They are less likely to constantly check in with him. They are less prone to delaying action until they get his approval.

I'll have much more to say about this in chapters 6 and 7. But suffice to say that these are critical differentiators of high performers today.

Adapt your behavior and teach others how to consume your time

Scott became quick to identify inefficient interaction norms and change them. He noticed, for example, that certain people tended to engage him in more meetings, or longer meetings, than was really necessary. Others tended to flood him with excessive emails. He recognized that for years, much like Reina, he had tolerated and even encouraged this behavior, just as he had unknowingly encouraged certain extroverted, chatty people to take up too much of his time, turning work interactions into social occasions.

He also saw that his constant interjections had conditioned his direct reports to perform at less than their full potential. Not a *lot* less, maybe—they were getting their work done, for sure—but they weren't coming through at the levels he knew they were capable of. Any limitations on performance, no matter how small, can add up quickly in today's workplaces, where we're all interdependent and many of us are working on multiple projects simultaneously. If people's less-than-peak effort on one initiative is forcing you to spend 5 percent more time on it than you should, that's bearable—you can live with that. But if the same thing is happening in all five of the initiatives you're working on, you're looking at a 25 percent impact on your time.

At first, Scott thought it would be impossible to change any of this. How could he make his interactions more efficient and raise his employees' work level without offending people? He found that when he tactfully made changes and clarified his expectations, no one was offended. He let people know that it was important that his contributions to discussions and meetings be brief and concise; people could have his time, but the amount would have to be limited, so the discussions would have to be carefully targeted. In some cases, he taught his direct reports to begin every discussion by stating its purpose.

The result: he is far less frequently pulled into minutiae that distracts him, because the people around him know how to use his time.

Allocating Appropriate Time

Think about when someone requests your time and you say yes: chances are you automatically schedule a half hour or an hour, or some larger multiple of thirty-minute blocks. Calendaring software assumes that's what you'll do and reinforces this thinking. But it doesn't have to be that way.

Set appropriate time for collaborative tasks

The more-efficient collaborators described reducing their time burden by thoughtfully allocating time on the basis of the true needs of the interaction. To increase the efficiency of their interactions, they also employ hard stops; they inform the people they're interacting with that the meeting will have to end at a certain time.

This is less about the specific tactics of calendaring than about the assumptions we make about allocating time. The top collaborators challenge their and others' assumptions.

Try establishing a norm of offering 50 percent of the meeting time that others ask of you. If you succeed in that, you will be able to buy back an enormous amount of time—often with no repercussions. One senior leader in my research took this to the extreme and cut in half every recurring meeting in his 14,000-person group. He did it as a gift to his employees leading into the holiday season. He laughed and told me, "Out of 14,000 people, I did not hear a single complaint."

Sometimes, though, longer can actually be better. In certain circumstances, such as when you are at the beginning of a project or are working with a distributed team in tackling a difficult or ambiguous task, consider doubling the meeting time—or halving the gap between meetings—to ensure that momentum is not lost. Sometimes it is more efficient to drive through to a solution in a two-hour meeting than to struggle to make things come together across a series of shorter meetings.

Developing Trust

The obscene numbers that we discovered in analyzing Scott when he was at his low point implied that his team had gotten into a rut of constantly checking with him. The team went to him almost obsessively, it seemed, to get his input or approval. This is common, and there are many reasons teams end up in this pattern. Sometimes teams get into checking routines because of a single past trauma.

Consider Jurgen. He was not a scary manager. He was a voluble, gregarious leader who enjoyed the company of his direct reports and often showed up at the nearby pub for after-hours drinks on Fridays. But everyone knew the story of what had happened to Karen, Anand, and Seth.

Just after the company had been acquired by a food-and-beverage giant, Jurgen was feeling particularly vulnerable under the new management. Karen, Anand, and Seth had been meeting regularly on their own to explore a new eco-friendly material for packaging frozen foods. Somehow a public radio station got wind of the project, and the trio (perhaps unwisely) gave interviews without Jurgen's permission.

This might not have been such a big deal except that the parent conglomerate had recently been embroiled in a legal fight in Germany over a similar packaging material because of allegations that it posed a health risk to pregnant mothers. Someone in the conglomerate's management heard the broadcast, and the irate CEO called Jurgen at home on a weekend.

From then on, Jurgen became more involved in the details of everyone's work—especially Karen, Anand, and Seth's. And over time he seemed to lose patience with them. They had been riding high, but after this incident they fell out of favor, getting noticeably less-desirable work. Karen and Anand quit. Seth stayed on, but he seemed to fade away.

Everyone liked and admired the trio; they had been among the most creative thinkers in the company. A few people kept in touch with Karen and Anand, so their post-resignation trials and tribulations became a running story in the workplace.

The effect on the dynamic between Jurgen and his team was noticeable. The lesson of Jurgen's response to his bosses' displeasure seemed to be: don't act independently. Check with Jurgen on everything. Both Jurgen and his team were soon overwhelmed with churn. They were swamped with approval requests, FYI memos, and check-in meetings, causing collaboration overload for all.

This is an extreme example, but an invisible fence of fear can be created just as easily through small moments, such as when employees detect disappointment in a leader's voice or body language, they are told in a meeting—even in a kind way—that they should have checked before taking action on some minor issue, or they are called out in a performance review for taking a trivial action that did not turn out well. Through these and other micro-moments, psychological safety slowly erodes, leading to tremendous inefficiency in collaborations.

This problem, at root, is a lack of trust. Jurgen's team members assumed that their manager didn't trust them, and for their part, they no longer trusted him to act reasonably or stand up for them.

Develop trust

You don't want people around you to be passive or to avoid taking action, generating ideas, or moving ahead independently. Nor do you want to be overwhelmed by churn as people come to you to triple-check everything. You want them to take risks. Prudent risks, yes, but risks. That's how you create a context of efficient collaboration.

Developing trust is never as easy as it sounds. Destroying trust *is* easy. It can be done in a single act, any day of the week, in public or in private. But building trust takes time and care. One misstep and you lose everything.

First, you must demonstrate—not just say—that you adhere to principles, such as the good of employees or the good of the company, that are larger than your own self-interest. In some cases, that might mean sticking your neck out for your employees, something Jurgen didn't do for his trio of creative thinkers. In other cases, it might mean refraining from wielding your expertise as an instrument of status; it's better to let others solve problems and discover mistakes in a way that creates ownership.

You must be authentic, because authenticity, sincerity, and believability foster trust. Yet being authentic doesn't mean blurting out what you really feel about your direct reports, especially if they've let you down.

Consider how you react to bad news or setbacks. Most leaders know they're not supposed to blow up, but often they don't realize that even subtle reactions such as slumping the shoulders, putting on a sour expression, or asking passive-aggressive questions can be just as effective as tantrums in training people not to take risks. If you are feeling upset for personal reasons, don't take it out on others, even in muted ways. Your employees watch your every move, are extremely perceptive, and rapidly transmit their impressions through the grapevine.

If you disagree with what people are doing, you must state your disagreement—agreeing with everyone and everything is no way to generate trust, because people understand that bosses must, at times, send stern messages. But make sure not to disagree in a way that could be seen as an attack on another person. Instead of saying, "That is a bad idea," say, "Given where we are trying to go, here is an alternative."

. . .

We have come a long way in the first half of this book. We have gone all the way around the left-hand side of the loop that I introduced in chapter 2 to see how altering our *beliefs, structures,* and *behaviors* can help free ourselves from overload.

By following the steps and "Coaching Breaks" in part 1, you can now buy back a significant chunk of your time. Earlier, I said that by transforming yourself into an essential collaborator, you can reclaim 18 percent to 24 percent of your time, or the equivalent of about one day per week. The way we discovered this figure is by comparing the most-efficient collaborators with people who were only average. We didn't even look at the least-efficient; instead, we focused on how much time you could reclaim if you moved from average efficiency to the level of the most-efficient collaborators.

OK, so I've given you the tools to become more efficient and regain a significant amount of your time. But now what? That's the question I will answer in part 2.

THE TAKEAWAY FOR YOU

Behaviors to Avoid Overload

As in previous chapters, I've taken all the practices that were discussed in this chapter and worded them as "I" statements so you can visualize applying the solutions to your own behavior. Check the box for the one or two that you think could be most helpful, given your current situation. Then ask someone who knows you well to indicate what they think could be most helpful to you, with your current behaviors in mind.

COLLABORATION PRACTICES: My meetings are focused on desired outcomes, include only those who need to be involved, and are efficient in structure and process.

☐ You
☐ Someone who knows you well

Solutions you could adopt

Establish healthy norms for before, during, and after meetings. These include: set expectations for desired outcomes; distribute preliminary information so that meeting time is spent on the best use of participants' expertise; employ appropriate structure, such as agenda and timeline, to meet clear objectives; send follow-up emails on commitments and next steps.

COLLABORATION PRACTICES: I write streamlined emails and encourage efficient norms of email use.

☐ You
☐ Someone who knows you well

Solutions you could adopt

Be more careful about format and organization of emails, use of email, and limiting disruptions. For example, establish norms for maximum length; efficiently clarify the "ask"; halt unnecessary cc'ing; avoid off-hours emailing; set reasonable norms on response time.

COLLABORATION PRACTICES: I use direct messaging to increase efficiency of established relationships.

☐ You
☐ Someone who knows you well

Solutions you could adopt

Use DM to spread and gather information quickly, conduct friendly interactions, and query people about their time constraints. But learn to ignore DM when in meetings or conversations so that you are present and not creating excessive collaborative demands.

COLLABORATION PRACTICES: I support virtual collaborations with rich media (for example, video and audio) and collaborative tools that enable colleagues to work on a single work product.

☐ You
☐ Someone who knows you well

Solutions you could adopt

Use videoconferencing and other rich technologies to brainstorm, integrate viewpoints, and ensure alignment. Employ tools that permit screen sharing or that enable participants to work together on a common document.

COLLABORATION PRACTICES: I draw people to collaborative work by giving status, envisioning joint success, diffusing ownership, and generating a sense of purpose and energy around an outcome.

☐ You
☐ Someone who knows you well

Solutions you could adopt

Co-create with influential stakeholders and others. Think about who will consume the output of your work, but also who could support your efforts. Seek to give first in interactions, to invoke a norm of reciprocity and trust.

COLLABORATION PRACTICES: I adapt my behavior and teach others how to consume my time rather than let inefficient norms develop and persist.

☐ You
☐ Someone who knows you well

Solutions you could adopt

Employ hard stops and help others understand how to make the best use of your limited bandwidth. Provide team members with resources and guidance, rather than setting yourself up as the person who knows all the answers and the "right" way of doing things. Coach people to be structured in how they approach you for help or input.

COLLABORATION PRACTICES: I allocate appropriate time for collaborative tasks rather than assume an hour or half hour is always needed.

☐ You

☐ Someone who knows you well

Solutions you could adopt

Challenge your assumptions about allocating time for interactions. A norm of offering 50 percent of the requested slot buys back an enormous amount of time. Don't fill time unnecessarily.

COLLABORATION PRACTICES: I develop trust so that people do not feel an excessive need to seek input or approvals.

☐ You

☐ Someone who knows you well

Solutions you could adopt

Show that you adhere to principles larger than your self-interest; let others solve problems in ways that build their sense of ownership; hold yourself and others accountable for acting with discretion, for doing what you say you will do, for being vulnerable and taking risks with ideas, and for showing concern for others.

PART TWO

USING YOUR NEW FREEDOM TO INCREASE PERFORMANCE AND WELL-BEING

P art 1 of this book showed you the invisible failures that are so often the result of collaboration overload. Overloaded people become gradually trapped and unable to engage with others in the most productive ways. When we're overloaded, we can't take the kinds of bold, creative actions that have significant impact on our careers, the organization, and the world.

Part 1 also showed that you can free yourself from overload by following the high performers' best practices and modifying your beliefs,

The infinite loop

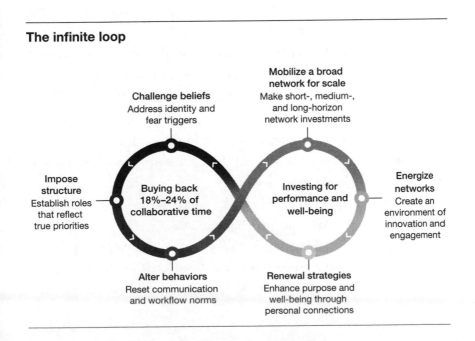

Challenge beliefs
Address identity and
fear triggers

**Mobilize a broad
network for scale**
Make short-, medium-,
and long-horizon
network investments

**Impose
structure**
Establish roles
that reflect
true priorities

**Buying back
18%–24% of
collaborative time**

**Investing for
performance and
well-being**

**Energize
networks**
Create an
environment of
innovation and
engagement

Alter behaviors
Reset communication
and workflow norms

Renewal strategies
Enhance purpose and
well-being through
personal connections

structures, and behaviors. These practices constitute the left-hand side of the infinite loop that I introduced in chapter 2.

Once you have bought back significant chunks of your time, you are on your way to mastering essential collaboration.

But essential collaboration is not just about freeing up time. The purpose of becoming more efficient isn't to reinvest your collaborative time the same way you did before. I've seen plenty of people reduce their overload only to take on more meetings, more emails, and more frenetic activity that, despite their best intentions, derails them, either sending them back to where they were or trading their old set of problems for new ones that undermine their careers and lives.[1]

The predictable derailers include becoming a bottleneck. This happens all too commonly when people who overcome overload go on to use their newfound time and energy to help others by jumping into more and more decisions. Although they may have positive intentions—they may enjoy a sense of accomplishment, like Scott in chapter 1, or they may feel it's important to avoid ambiguity—they end up becoming choke points. They get so involved in every decision that they deprive their employees of challenges that would allow them to grow.

Others—again, starting with positive intentions—become what I call *biased learners, disconnected leaders,* or *formalists.* Biased learners allow certain people—such as those who are physically nearby or who have a similar functional background or common values—to disproportionately influence their learning and decision-making. When successful people are promoted, they continue to turn to 60 percent to 70 percent of their trusted ties to brainstorm or test ideas. Trust is a good thing, right? But often the perspectives of these trusted friends become less and less relevant in the new context.

Disconnected leaders try to project a laudable image of knowledge and decisiveness when in fact they have knowledge gaps and skills deficiencies that they need to address. Successful people face many transition points—promotions, new roles, role expansions, or side projects in areas where they have only partial expertise—and often there is little or no time to develop the needed new skills. In trying to project their image, disconnected leaders don't admit their shortcomings and thus fail to cover their skill gaps through their networks.

Formalists see their networks through a hierarchical lens. In trying to follow the organization's rules, they rely too heavily on the formal structure as a map of how work gets done. They don't realize that the lines and boxes on formal org charts can mask or distort the underlying networks and collaborations that are the true currency of execution. This myopia, which particularly impacts people who are more junior, leads people to fail to understand or leverage the power of informal networks. As a result, they miss important levers of influence.

The key to avoiding these derailers and achieving impact is what you do with your liberation from overload. The beliefs, structures, and behaviors that you learned in chapters 3, 4, and 5 constitute a force field around you that protects you from overload and has given you the gift of more time to reinvest. How are you going to put this precious freedom to the best possible use? How are you going to achieve maximum impact?

Once you've bought back a sizable chunk of your time, it's critical to shift your focus toward creating personal connections that help you achieve greater performance, impact, and well-being. That's the other half of the battle, and the other half of the infinite loop.

As you will see in part 2, the best practices on the right-hand side of the loop lead to reputational capital and a greater flow of good things toward you. A greater sense of well-being and a reputation for being an energizer—a person others want to follow—give you the clout to set clearer boundaries and push back on work that doesn't add value. That's why the two sides of the loop are interdependent: the benefits on the right side enable you to further reduce collaboration overload on the left side.

So, follow me into the right-hand side of the loop, where you will learn to use your network to accomplish things of greater substance and to show up for others, the organization, and yourself in a way that is sustainable.

6

Networks of Successful People

"Networks matter here more than anywhere else I have ever been," I was proudly told by the president of one of the world's most beloved consumer-products organizations. "If you're an employee and you don't figure this out, it just doesn't matter how smart you are or what you have done before."

As a network researcher, I was excited to hear those words. An understanding of networks, I knew, was the key to understanding effective collaboration, as we will see in this half of the book. Had I found a like-minded colleague, someone with influence who was ready to put network ideas into play for a massive organization?

"Great!" I replied. "What kinds of things do you do to help people cultivate the right connections?"

"From day one, we encourage people to learn the culture," the executive said. "Leaders come in to speak to each incoming class. We make clear the importance of building a big network. And we hold a series of social events so the newcomers can mingle and meet their new peers. We also encourage everyone to join associations and be involved with their community."

I kept smiling, but my inner voice kicked in (I have learned, over the years, to hold it at bay): *This has nothing to do with helping people understand and replicate what high performers do through networks. This is just shooting blindly—telling people something is critical and then saying, "Good luck storming the castle."*

This was yet another company that failed to understand how successful people build and tap personal networks. Just the week before, I had heard the same story at a global insurance organization. A couple of weeks before that, at a leading software organization. Before that, at a highly respected professional-services organization. In fact, I have this same conversation thirty or more times a year. Leaders say they recognize that networks are critical to success, but they do nothing to help clarify what a good network looks like or how successful people create their network connections.

This lack of helpful specificity is not just the domain of organizations. Look at today's social technologies and online platforms: They offer rapid means to connect and collaborate with a dizzying array of people, but what does *good* networking look like?

What do high performers do? What network strategies distinguish the people who stay for years in their jobs from those who run into trouble and leave early? What aspects of connectivity distinguish those who are happy and sustainable in their careers?

Network Diversity

The starting point for answering these questions is the pioneering work of Ron Burt, who showed that people with noninsular networks—those that encompass a diversity of perspectives, values, and expertise—are more successful.[1] These structurally diverse networks often bridge expertise domains, cultures, geographical regions, functional areas, and other pockets of mastery and opinion. Interactions with people who are in different clusters of a network enable us to see problems and opportunities in novel ways.

Burt's work showed that people who build these kinds of networks are promoted more rapidly. Other researchers have shown that non-insular networks are associated with higher pay and greater career mobility. My own work in the Connected Commons across several hundred organizations has consistently found that noninsular networks predict higher individual performance.

Visually, the idea can be portrayed through playing the game Six Degrees of Kevin Bacon and comparing Bacon with an actor such as Jim Carrey (see figure 6-1). Bacon turns out to be a well-connected actor in the movie universe not so much because of the number of films he has been in as the number of genres. Whereas Carrey and most other actors stay within one or two genres, Bacon has appeared in

FIGURE 6-1

Six Degrees of Kevin Bacon

Noninsular versus insular networks

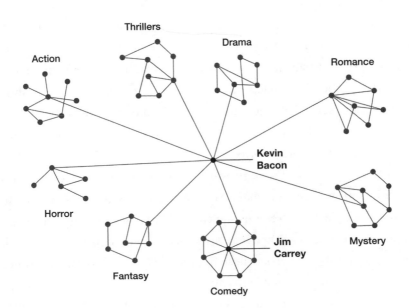

Source: Thanks to Wayne Baker for the discussion that led to this graphic.

many more, and it is the bridging ties across genres—or clusters in the network—that make him central in the movie universe.

I am not saying Bacon is a good or bad actor—you can make your own call on his cinematic prowess. Rather, the point is that people in companies who maintain a structurally diverse network like Bacon's tend to be more successful.

In contrast, when I reference an insular network, I mean one more like Carrey's, where the people connected to him are also heavily connected to each other. Of course, the pattern in real life is never perfect like the graphic, but as leaders evolve, if they allow their meetings, email distribution lists, and workflows to excessively involve the same people over and over, they tend to become insular and less innovative in their work.

The finding that a structurally diverse network is key to personal performance is one of the foundational discoveries in social-network research. Many other researchers, such as Wayne Baker, Herminia Ibarra, and Linda Hill, have shed further light on network structure and helped all of us see how knowledge work is enhanced by structurally diverse networks.

Despite clear evidence that diverse networks work, people struggle to figure out *how* to build them. Leaders ask: Should you continually network with people outside your circle? Do certain relationships matter more than others? Probably the most common questions I get about this are: Does it really make sense to spend time building a structurally diverse network? Doesn't the specific work I'm doing determine which people I need to interact with?

To begin providing real answers, I conducted two interview studies with 260 women and men. My approach was to assess successful people—people who are consistently high performers and who score higher on measures of thriving, resilience, career satisfaction, or well-being. I wanted to see what these people did through networks to perform well and be sustainable in their careers.

The process of conducting these interviews was very illuminating in itself.

Seeing the Invisible Social Ecology
of High Performers

First, I would usually need a few tries to get each interviewee on the phone. I came to expect that five minutes before the allotted time, I would get an email from the interviewee's assistant saying there had been a dire emergency and asking if it would be possible to postpone. (It was amazing how many dire emergencies came up in the lives of these individuals—sick children, dental crises, deaths in the family. Definitely a statistical anomaly. I'm pretty sure some of the deaths happened more than once.)

I wasn't surprised. These were high performers, and the call with the academic was clearly their lowest priority. Ultimately, I wore them down with my persistence and finally would get them on the phone. I would tell them that I was interested in hearing about their career-defining successes, the times when they accomplished things that put them on their current paths. Then I added, "But what I want to talk about is not what you did individually. What I want you to reflect on is how your network enabled you to see the opportunities to organize and pursue the initiatives and to implement them efficiently."

The response was almost always: "Great! I have a good one for you." The person would be off to the races, but not in the way I hoped. Instead, they'd tell me a story that had nothing to do with other people. It was entirely their own valiant efforts that made things happen. If others were involved, they usually served as obstacles for our hero to overcome.

Because many of the interviewees were high-level executives, it would take me a while to be able to step in. At about the five-minute mark, I would ask, "Why this thing? Of all the things that you could have spent time on at this point in your life, why this?"

"Oh," the person would say. And after a moment's reflection: "It started with an interaction with _____" and the interviewee would name a person in his or her network. "And then _____" (another person). "And then _____." "And later _____." Eventually, the interviewee would acknowledge that what had really mattered was the integration of the interactions with all these people.

Before the interviewee could build up a new head of steam on the solo narrative, I would say, "Well, this took you into new areas, right? Exposed gaps for you in technical, market, political, or cultural domains, right? What did you do in those domains?"

"Oh." Another pause. "I talked to _____" (another person). "And _____." And _____."

"Huh," I would say. "Tell me, did you have any moments where you had to pivot? And did still others play important roles in that?"

"Oh yeah. This happened at two key points . . ."

And on it would go as we explored the person's success not as a product of their individual efforts but as a product of the network. (See the Coaching Break, "Recognizing Your Own Social Ecology.")

The interviewees didn't resist the recasting of their stories at all. To the contrary, they were often very thoughtful and forthcoming once I had prompted them a couple of times. In fact, around 75 percent of the calls ended up going long, as the interviewees valued the experience of reexamining their successes in this new light. What had been a five-minute account of a supposedly single-handed success became a much longer tale involving a rich social ecology. (Now it was the *next* people on their schedule, the people after me, who got the excuses about the sick children, dental crises, and extended family member passing away.)

When I tell this story, I am sometimes asked why it took all that prompting to get the interviewees to recognize the social ecologies critical to their achievements. Are successful people arrogant? I don't think so. Rather, I think everyone is just limited cognitively. If we can't remember a phone number for twenty seconds, how can we be expected to recall all the interactions we experience over the life of a long project?

This is a critical point. Network interactions that enable career-defining successes are in a sense invisible to us. Cognitively we put ourselves in the center of our success narratives and recall more easily the actions we took and less fluidly the ways relationships shaped our success. In fact, we are psychologically wired to attribute successes to our own behaviors, and failures to others' actions. As a result, we learn to re-apply behaviors that we think make us successful but do not consciously learn and recreate the network interactions that also play a critical role.

Like the air we breathe, these connections are essential but in important ways unseen.

The Wisdom of the Trenches

The upshot of the interviews was understanding that advice on networking well is sorely lacking. Traditional guidance too often centers on how to use connections to find a job, get venture funding, or sell a product or service. All of that is important, to be sure. But the kind of networking that generates a large volume of surface-level interactions so you can get a job, or hustle up funds or prospects, is not reflective of the ways more-successful people in my research initiated and leveraged networks to deliver career-defining accomplishments.

In particular, the quantitative research from the Connected Commons shows that if you want to be successful, a bigger network is typically *not* better. This is a striking finding, especially given the number of companies that take pride in encouraging their employees to build large networks and the number of self-help books on networking that start with the central premise that a big network is a good one.

True, in transactional fields such as residential real estate, network size does make a difference. But, generally, it is not the critical factor distinguishing satisfied, thriving high performers from other people in their organizations. Managing a big, sprawling network is time consuming, and that time sink can actually end up generating collaboration overload and hurting performance.

Another surprising discovery was that very few of the successful people I studied followed the classic advice to intentionally create structurally diverse networks. Despite the demonstrated links between network diversity and achievement, there just wasn't a lot of proactive development

Recognizing Your Own Social Ecology

Think about one of your successful projects and list key moments in which you took action to drive that success. That's step one.

Then, on a blank piece of paper, draw a horizontal line to represent the project's timeline, left to right.

On the far left, above the line, list a person or multiple people who helped you see the possibilities in this project. Below that, list people who were critical sources of expertise or resources in the project's inception.

At the midpoint, above the line, list people who helped you understand how to position your ideas, how to influence others, or how to obtain resources or approvals. Below that, list people who entered midstream and changed your perspective on the project or whom you relied on to cover skill or expertise gaps.

On the far right, above the line, list people who helped you pivot or adapt when a challenge arose or the project direction shifted. Below that, list anyone who gave you personal support during the project, such as letting you vent or discuss problems in ways that helped you get back on track.

Finally, review the entire timeline and consider one or more points where serendipity played a role—where you ran into someone unexpectedly and it ended up helping the project in one way or another.

Now go back and look at the list of your own actions that you wrote at the beginning of this exercise and compare that with the rich ecosystem you have just sketched out. Telling your story from the network vantage point requires a shift in perception; it's like in physics, where a packet of energy can be seen as either a particle or a wave.

Notice the variety of connections across your timeline. Often, different ties matter at different points in a project's life. The development and leverage of these connections distinguish the top performers. Use this timeline to see where gaps could be filled in future efforts.

Recognizing your own social ecology

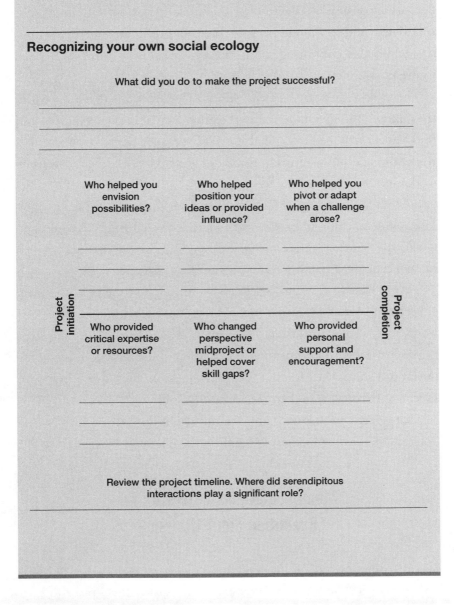

What did you do to make the project successful?

_____

_____

_____

Who helped you envision possibilities?

Who helped position your ideas or provided influence?

Who helped you pivot or adapt when a challenge arose?

Project initiation

Project completion

Who provided critical expertise or resources?

Who changed perspective midproject or helped cover skill gaps?

Who provided personal support and encouragement?

Review the project timeline. Where did serendipitous interactions play a significant role?

of these networks by, for example, stocking networks with assets such as brokers who can link to disparate groups. But these people did create network diversity in very interesting ways across planning horizons and work demands.

The reality in organizations, I found, is that successful people do network—constantly—but not "by the book." They network intuitively, reflexively, and in unique ways that respond to immediate opportunities, while also cultivating connections over the long term that create future possibilities.

They know they need specific kinds of interactions that will ensure the quality of their solutions and the efficiency of implementation, and they know they need to capitalize rapidly on short-term opportunities, while also sculpting future possibilities through specific kinds of network initiation and development.

So, they make a leap of faith, letting go of control, embracing ambiguity, and reaching out early—actions that may at times expose them to ridicule but that lead to the development of diverse networks, which in turn create the conditions for outstanding success.

This is what you might call the wisdom of the trenches—the tacit, experiential knowledge that successful people generate by using networks to get their work done. The interviewees learned to take steps that were risky, time consuming, and sometimes selfless, to generate outsized results. They figured this out largely on their own, rarely with specific guidance from their organizations.

That doesn't mean you have to figure it out on your own, of course. You can take the knowledge of what they did and apply it to your own life.

Medium-Horizon Networks for Execution and Efficiency

Successful people take a nuanced approach to networks that depends on the work's time horizon. For many, the most natural place to start building an effective network is with *medium-horizon* projects—those career-defining (or at least career-enhancing) initiatives that are happening now and are expected to unfold over the next few months or so.

Most of us have at least one and usually three or four core, medium-horizon projects or strategic objectives that are critical to our future success. Examples might include a restructuring project for a consulting client, moving a new product through a development process, or generating software that extends functionality for a given code base. It is important to define these efforts and make sure they are truly core; there should be no more than three or four core priorities. The scope, objective, and time frame of these initiatives should also have become relatively firm and stable.

These medium-horizon work streams dictate what kinds of connections are critical for effective and efficient delivery of results. Medium-horizon network investments around one or more core projects or priorities are critical to successful people's ability to scale their work and implement it efficiently. By cultivating the right set of connections proactively for medium-horizon work, successful individuals are far less likely to hit points of resistance that derail their efforts.

The investments pay off tremendously in producing results that are larger than any one person's individual capacity. And they further build a network of trust and reputation for delivery that pays dividends in future efforts.

In my research, the medium-horizon work of the interviewees proved to be a showcase for how successful people craft their networks. They do this along four critical fronts:

- They cultivate connections to break out of narrow ideas.

- They envision projects as sets of activities for a network, rather than as linear lists of tasks.

- They use their networks to fill their knowledge gaps.

- And they connect with influencers (including resisters) to gain perspective and efficiency.

So let's look in detail at this medium-horizon work.

Cultivating connections to break out of narrow ideas

I have explored more than 250 career-defining accomplishments in great detail, and in every single one, the successful men and women experienced critical pivot moments that happened because of contributions from their networks. *Every single one.* In contrast, when sufficient interview time allowed—and people were comfortable sharing stories of failures—the interviewees often pointed to network insularity and developing solutions in isolation as keys to failure. This is natural. As work streams become established, we begin working to specific time frames and cadences with other people, and this can create insular informational environments that generate only narrow, familiar ideas. (See the Coaching Break, "Hearing Crickets.")

The more-successful women and men in my research used their networks to puncture this idea bubble. How? They proactively initiated contact with people who could help them with their evolving projects or strategic priorities. These included technical experts who could help reframe and improve a solution's efficiency, as well as other knowledgeable people who could help validate the effectiveness of the work. In many cases, the high performers systematically reached out to downstream customers of their solutions to get valuable user feedback. Rather than charge ahead with a plan that their teams felt good about, they were much more likely to identify components of their solutions that might be less than ideal and proactively engage their network to enhance solutions.

They also built serendipity into their lives to help surface possibilities that they would not have known to seek out. You can't effectively break out of narrow ideas simply by reaching out on your own; you are held back by the limits of your knowledge and the span of your network. You need to invite and embrace serendipity.

In telling their stories, many of the interviewees at first unconsciously skipped over the serendipitous occurrences that had influenced their performance. It took a few questions to get people to recall these instances, but it turned out there were plenty of them. In fact, I was

Hearing Crickets

It's crucial to adapt our networks to yield the best outcome and not fall into comfortable or convenient patterns of interacting with people we trust or like or who are easily accessible to us.

Consider Cristal, an engineering graduate of a leading university with over a decade of success in a well-regarded organization. As a rising star, Cristal was tapped by her CEO to lead the commercialization of a product she had helped create. All conditions pointed to success on program launch—top talent was placed on the project, executive support was strong, and funding was established. But nine months later, she was looking for a new job, because nothing was going as expected. There was poor coordination among the three work streams in the sixty-four-person part-time team—sales and marketing, product development, and research—and the team wasn't hitting its deadlines.

Cristal's impression was that the sales and marketing and product-development people weren't making enough time for the project. "They slow the work and hurt the morale of others who are putting in the time," she said. The sales and product development people also seemed uninterested in the research group's ideas. "We would present really well-thought-out actions and get pushback or just crickets."

People on the team said that even though the project was explicitly a commercialization effort, Cristal overemphasized research at the expense of the other functions. They weren't wrong: my network analysis showed that she interacted mainly with research-oriented people—colleagues she knew and trusted and with whom she shared values and perspectives—while having only the most superficial interactions with people in sales and product development. The numbers were

(continued)

stark: the network of people she regularly spoke with included seventeen from research, two from sales, and five from product development, of whom two were included only because they sought her out. Some 73 percent of her interactions were with people in research.

As Cristal and I looked over the numbers, it became evident to her that her close ties to her research colleagues and friends—her community—had skewed her perspective, leading her to think about the project mainly along research lines. She recognized that she had fallen victim to the derailer of being a *biased learner* (see the introduction to part 2). She had held on to comfortable, trusted, validating relationships at the expense of a broader perspective. Unfortunately, she discovered this so late in the game that there was no way to undo the damage.

Reflect for a moment on disproportionately influential spheres in your own network—perhaps people you trust, are proximate to, or who share similar expertise. Of course, you do not want to drop these people from your network, but you do want to balance their influence by recognizing this reliance and cultivating new connections into spheres that will help you have a more accurate perspective.

Leaders typically have been advised on many, many decision-making biases that exist in the six inches between our ears. But oddly enough, we all still fall prey to phenomenal biases in how the information enters our brain to begin with through our networks.

floored by how often serendipitous moments impacted the trajectory of career-defining successes.

The interviews revealed that serendipitous events make up a larger part of our success than most of us realize, and that the most-successful people benefit greatly from them. Serendipity is partly a matter of luck, but the most-accomplished people have a knack for *generating* serendipity.

In the interviews, I would ask, "Do you manufacture serendipity?" The idea may seem like an oxymoron, but over and over, people said yes. You can't force fortuitous discoveries (they would tell me), but you *can* systematically pursue serendipity by creating routines for exploring ideas across the network and using serendipitous moments well. (See the Coaching Break, "Making Serendipity Happen.")

Envisioning projects as sets of activities for a network

High performers see the network as a fluid extension of their own expertise, and they see the network as magnifying what they can do. The key is to envision projects and opportunities as sets of activities for a network, not as linear lists of tasks for you to accomplish. Most successful people described key inflection points in their careers where they ceased to see work as streams of activities that they needed to accomplish and stopped trying to fit tasks into existing roles, teams, or processes. Instead, they began to envision how tasks could be mapped onto capabilities in their networks. In turn, this enabled them to see possibilities to leverage talent broadly.

I am aware that this is a subtle point. In fact, it took me a while to identify this as one of the main ways people succeed through networks. I kept getting hints of it, but after a while, a few of the interviewees crystallized it for me.

One was a manager I'll call Margaux, who has PhD and MBA degrees and has sculpted a role in a global pharma company taking ideas and processes that work in one area and adapting and scaling them for other areas. It's smart that the company has someone doing that kind of work, right? And Margaux, who has a wide-ranging mind and loves crossing business and research boundaries, does it very well.

Margaux showed me how she thinks and works. One day she was learning about people working on an experimental mass-spectrometry blood test for early-stage Alzheimer's disease and had the sudden insight that this relatively inexpensive and noninvasive technology might be useful in other parts of the company.

COACHING BREAK

Making Serendipity Happen

Chance is chance and luck is luck, but you can take steps to commingle people and ideas with the aim of stimulating serendipitous occurrences. All it requires is an openness to unforeseen directions and a few systematic behaviors. Interviewees told me they created routines for exploring ideas across the network and using serendipitous moments well.

Some of the practices include:

- Walking to the office or going out for lunch or coffee by a different route as often as possible, just for a change of scenery

- While walking to lunch or coffee with colleagues, stealing five minutes of their time to shoot the breeze or discuss new ideas

- Setting aside time each week to meet one or two new colleagues or have exploratory conversations with people

- Telling people about an idea or a problem you are trying to solve—asking how they would tackle it or who they would bring in to help

- Using networking tools to prompt new thinking—for example, reviewing LinkedIn for updates on contacts' interests and roles and searching for past contacts that could be rejuvenated for new purposes

- Volunteering for activities or events that bring you into contact with new people, such as giving tours or participating in onboarding programs

In order to see where it might apply, she needed to better understand the kinds of problems that other areas of the company were facing. Rather than view this as a challenge for just herself or her team, she dealt with it as a network challenge. She tapped a range of people with relevant knowledge.

"It's important to be able to identify how your local space might have tie-ins with other parts of the organization," she said. "I try to hop across networks to get to other areas, other expertise. Each person is a conduit to see how much further we can go to have a broader discussion."

One research group expressed interest, but the technology turned out not to map well to the group's work. "The initial conversation was along the lines of 'While this tool is a good start, it doesn't really address all our needs,'" Margaux said. "But then we had a conversation about which other groups might have needs that would be met by the test. We brainstormed who else we could reach out to."

The "aha" moment came when a group working on the metabolic disease amyloidosis expressed interest because the test screened for amyloid protein, which plays a role in amyloidosis. Margaux's MO is to see where opportunities exist and to view possibilities or projects as elements or pieces to be mapped onto various people. Using this network, she tries to understand the problem and potential solutions. Then she'll work with an initial group to get their framing of the problem space and branch out to find other potential players or stakeholders.

Do you see what I mean about the wisdom of the trenches? Margaux doesn't think about network structure per se. She doesn't focus on a taxonomy of roles. And she doesn't think of her network as permanent and unchanging. Instead, she networks in relation to her specific work. The work itself dictates key network connections. Margaux thinks about the work and who could inform it, lift it, support it, and extend it. Then she goes to those people and develops connections based on shared interests. Understanding that this is a human community, she lets her feelings of appreciation, admiration, gratitude, and liking shine through.

Of course, Margaux can do this because she has not allowed herself to get collaboratively overwhelmed. The very first thing that goes out the door when people pass thresholds of overload are these kinds of inter-actions in networks that generate innovation and scale. Because work, in the end, is about the specific work we do. We network not to build networks, but to make the work go better and to have greater impact.

Throughout, the more-successful people in my research would envision ways that greater results could be produced by leveraging others and engage those groups in a mutually beneficial way. Or they would see that work coming to them could be a developmental opportunity for others on their teams and shift tasks in ways that enabled them to be more efficient, while at the same time building capability in their teams.

In myriad ways, this ability to see work and the network simultaneously was key to how they were able to scale accomplishments in collaboratively intense work.

Using networks to fill knowledge gaps

Usually, core projects create skill gaps. Failing to recognize these gaps—or acknowledging them privately but trying to bluff our way through them publicly—often results in being blindsided at some point. As a rule, successful people more readily admit their shortcomings and find people whose knowledge and skills fill the gaps.

One of the successful leaders in my study personified this approach wonderfully. He was stepping into a new role to replace an externally hired executive who had flamed out after nine months. Gary was promoted from within and was presumed to be a wonderful choice; he was well regarded, had run the major business line in this unit, and with a twenty-plus-year tenure, had a clear understanding of the culture. Yet as soon as he started, he began hearing terms he didn't understand. The terminology flew by quickly, and he didn't want to interrupt the high-pressure conversations for vocabulary lessons during the first-impressions phase.

As the days passed, his colleagues and employees seemed to get the sense that he knew what they were talking about. He could have encouraged this misimpression by keeping his mouth shut, but he saw the situation as an opportunity to recognize and supplement his knowledge gaps, which were much greater than he had supposed they would be.

Gary got a notebook and began jotting down every unfamiliar word. At the end of the first month, he met with his team, took out the notebook, and said, "There are thirty-three terms I've heard that I don't understand." He asked the team to help him fill in the gaps. Many of the terms turned out to be critical to his ability to make good decisions in the new role, and the team was quick to find experts for Gary to rely on.

Successful people tapped networks in different ways to supplement these gaps. The world is too complex today to master every element of any project of substance. It is key to reflect on gaps—typically that occur in technical knowledge, market awareness, cultural understanding, political dynamics, or leadership capabilities—and find ways to supplement your unique value-add through connections.

Connecting with influencers (and resisters) to gain perspective and efficiency

This strategy includes engaging with formal decision makers as well as informal opinion leaders to cultivate influence without authority. Early outreach is commonly a key factor in successful people's lives. These efforts often head off catastrophic failures in which a project might be halted by a formal committee or key stakeholder.

Equally important, these connections make implementation far more efficient. The best connectors use their networks to quickly defend and marshal support for their ideas. They can accomplish in one or two meetings what it takes others five or more meetings to do.

Formal influencers to consider are those who have decision-making authority over resources such as time, talent, or funding, as well as those who occupy roles where misalignment in objectives can erode team success. Identify relevant formal stakeholders and customize your engagement strategy with them on the basis of their unique needs. A simple but effective exercise is to role-play a meeting with them and take their perspective.

One leader in life sciences described engaging key financial sponsors early on—months ahead of the formal planning and funding process—to make sure that the tasks coming into his unit were well aligned with his employees' aspirations. He did this not with a detailed slide deck but with a single slide and rich conversations focused on possibilities. "That approach allows us both to create streams of work that better align with our respective needs," he said.

The key is to look for opportunities to shape the work where doing so will build vital capabilities and increase the team's engagement. But this is often counterintuitive to people who think they need to perfect the idea—or bulletproof the deck of slides—before outreach.

As for engaging *informal* opinion leaders, the high performers spent time identifying and engaging those whose perspective had a disproportionate impact on others' acceptance of an idea or rollout of a new program or process. They were quick to engage these people in ideation and solution-development processes so that their teams incorporated the opinion leaders' thinking and obtained their support early. The result was that the high performers boosted the efficiency and effectiveness with which their work moved forward. Their projects were less likely to derail at high-stakes approval points.

When evaluating how the network could benefit your work, consider two kinds of influencers: first, those who, by virtue of their connections with disparate parts of the organization, can position your ideas in ways that various teams or units will accept. And, second, those who are listened to by a large number of people; these individuals often dictate how others in a unit or geography feel about your initiative and so have a disproportionate effect on implementation success.

Successful people are often far more likely to reach out to positive people who will spread energy and enthusiasm for an idea. But the key differentiator lies with their greater propensity to proactively identify influential resisters and naysayers. This is a consistently prominent characteristic of high performers. Good collaborators are really persistent in locating and engaging negative opinion leaders early.

Sometimes the naysayers are curmudgeonly people who are de-energizers or overly critical. But more often they are colleagues who have different priorities driven by functional commitments, incentives, or what they personally value in their work. Finding resisters when plans are still in flux might seem risky or even counterproductive, but often it dramatically influences success. Don't shy away from contacting these people directly.

Deliberately engaging influencers is an often overlooked but critical driver of success. Per one financial-services leader: "Probably 75 percent of the final product features emerge through all the adjustments in implementation. You have to build time into your calendar and forums to message benefits and rationale for your program of work, obtain feedback in pilots, and communicate actions you have taken on that feedback."

Consider Leo. He was just a few years into his postcollege career at a top technology firm when he was assigned to work on a product extension that would help business customers hit key financial goals.

Leo figured out who might oppose the plan and connected with them early on. "I reached out to two people who I knew were skeptical, and then in a series of meetings that also included my positive energizers, I asked for their input," he said. "This was critical on two levels for me. First, the ideas I got from the skeptical people were central. Second, just getting their input early got them on my side."

At several select points, he sought advice from his boss and skip-level manager. The key in these interactions was coming to them not with a perfected plan but rather with something that was 70 percent directionally sound. "I would show them I had done the work and had a plan," he said, "but then create space for them to help mold it too. I got great ideas this way and also their support." I have heard that some people take twenty years to figure out that this approach is often better than going in with a fully detailed plan and slide deck. By leaving some room to co-create, you get formal sponsors' support, and the sponsors tell others about the work as if it were their idea. The payoff is immense in speeding implementation.

Leo carefully turned to his network to implement the solution he developed through his network. He proactively obtained sponsorships from key people. As the project grew, he included people who represented various customers, types of work, and areas of operations. He

COACHING BREAK

Key Network Investments for Medium Horizon

Reflect on a core project or strategic imperative in your work, one that is substantial to your current and future success. Identify connections in the list that you should initiate, rejuvenate, or tap into over the coming three to six months.

Project or strategic imperative:

_____

_____

_____

_____

Cultivate connections to break out of narrow ideas. Identify domain experts, technical specialists, and downstream stakeholders or consumers whom you should engage as work evolves.

_____

_____

_____

_____

Use networks to fill knowledge gaps. Reflect on technical skills, market knowledge, cultural understanding, or political-awareness

also drew in potential allies and advisers, as well as network brokers who could bridge internal silos and external groups and connectors who would socialize ideas and be conduits of information.

. . .

The lesson in the medium horizon is the importance of intentional network development around one or more core projects or priorities.

gaps related to your work. Identify people or kinds of people who can help you supplement or address gaps.

_____

_____

_____

_____

Envision projects as sets of activities for a network. Identify activities that you could distribute in your network. Look to diffuse ownership early, create mutual wins, and advance development objectives. Remove yourself from the center of the network.

_____

_____

_____

_____

Connect with influencers to gain perspective and efficiency. Reflect on formal leaders and stakeholders—informal influencers and energizers who will spread the word, and naysayers or detractors who might slow diffusion.

_____

_____

_____

_____

The first step is to define these efforts and make sure they are truly core. The second step is to initiate connectivity in the four categories discussed earlier to ensure effectiveness of the idea and efficiency of its implementation. These investments give you leverage and scale and add to your reputation. (See the Coaching Break, "Key Network Investments for Medium Horizon.")

Network investments for the medium-term horizon are powerful; they enable you to innovate and execute in ways far beyond your own abilities. But, obviously, not everything happens in the medium term. Some of the most challenging work we do involves very short horizons or very long horizons.

Network Diversity from Conversations across Three Time Horizons

A central insight from my interviews—and hopefully one you can see in your own life through the "Recognizing Your Own Social Ecology" coaching break earlier in this chapter—emerged through the consistent ways successful people cultivate and tap networks across short-, medium-, and long-term planning horizons. Connections within and across these horizons provide a critical foundation of network diversity and performance. But each horizon is qualitatively different in both the nature of the conversations and the network's benefits to performance.

As we've seen, medium-horizon interactions are usually defined by projects' needs and are central to effective and efficient execution. Most of us live and experience work in the medium horizon. Streams of work with somewhat defined objectives, timelines, and interdependencies structure network actions. Here we see that high performers are prone to be proactive in shaping a more successful set of collaborations. But they also cultivate connections in two other ways that are critical to success: short-horizon and long-horizon interactions that turn out to be equally critical yet more likely to get overlooked as one deals with the present (see figure 6-2).

Short-horizon interactions are typically shaped by a presenting opportunity, and they are critical to innovation. *Long-horizon* interactions are forms of exploration that are pivotal for laying the groundwork for future success. These time horizons work as a system. They inform each other. Working across them is what enables successful people to simultaneously deliver more-substantive results and create efficient and innovative networks that fuel future success.

Three time horizons

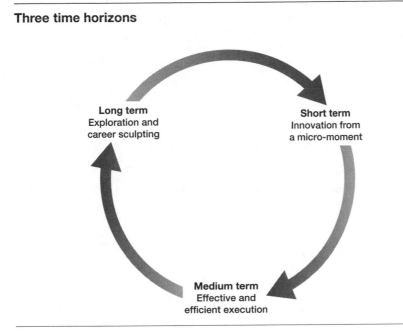

Long term
Exploration and
career sculpting

Short term
Innovation from
a micro-moment

Medium term
Effective and
efficient execution

The Short Horizon: Innovation from Micro-Moments

Some of our most pressing challenges are the most immediate. In this horizon, our network choices are usually determined by the nature of a request made of us or the opportunity we envision at a point in time. For example, we get a request from a manager, senior stakeholder, client, or colleague, or we hear of an opportunity to apply our expertise in a given technology to a new problem the company is facing.

At this nascent stage, people are not really thinking about supplementing skill gaps and connecting with influencers. That happens only after a project or stream of work has started to take hold for the medium horizon.

In the short term, it really is about emergent innovation—about reframing the problem or solution space and starting conversations with others who might be involved if things move to the medium horizon. These are often fleeting opportunities where choices made in a micro-moment open up or close down possibilities. Career-defining successes hinge on our posture toward micro-moments. If you have allowed yourself to become collaboratively overloaded, you are far less likely to recognize and take action on these micro-moments. Yet time and time again, my interviewees' career-defining accomplishments could be traced back to these moments.

Micro-moments tend to take two forms. First is a request—and of course, a request never lands on an empty plate: requests always hit us when we are busy, so our decision in the moment is a critical one. Do we:

1. Say no?

2. Cringe but hunker down to address the request as efficiently as possible?

3. Reframe the request to provide a more comprehensive solution that involves others?

The second kind of micro-moment occurs when we envision a possibility—for example, when an idea sparks as we pass someone in the hallway (or see them on a video conference), we gain a unique insight when someone pops up on LinkedIn, or we have a "doorway moment"— a thought as we are leaving a meeting. These ideas are usually just vague intuitions, and they never occur when we are sitting idly with an hour of free time. Rather, they happen when we are late for the next meeting or still have a mountain of email to address. Responses typically include:

1. Discarding the idea

2. Making a note to follow up

3. Maybe capitalizing on the micro-moment to explore the possibility while the idea—and the interaction with your colleague—is fresh

What is your typical response to both kinds of micro-moments? People who opt for choices one or two in both lists of actions—in other words, who choose not to take a more expansive route—end up accomplishing less-substantive outcomes, and their networks remain more insular than those who default to option three.

The high performers more frequently choose the third option on both lists. They have a greater tendency to recognize these opportunities as possible inflection points. They are able to pause and engage their networks to follow up on and explore these potentially fruitful ideas. Through tapping their networks broadly—and early—they envision solutions with greater impact and create positive reputations. They win by simultaneously accomplishing more and building social capital for themselves.

Over time, the results they produce elevate and distinguish them from colleagues who are similarly intelligent and working often longer hours. Many of the successful women and men in my research were able to trace their career-defining accomplishments to pursuits of half-formed ideas during micro-moments.

Harvesting a micro-moment

For most of us, one of the most challenging aspects of network investments in the micro-moment is that they are too easily put off or ignored, especially during times of ambiguity or feverish activity. And, to be fair, it is not as if people get fired for failing to take the more expansive route in a micro-moment. They usually produce a satisfactory result but not one that is as significant or that builds social capital in the same way as the high performers.

It is important to react quickly to these fleeting opportunities, for three reasons. First, as the network and peoples' priorities change, your chance to do something big might come and go more quickly than you realize. Second, with our suspect memories, we lose these moments in the ether a lot more than we realize. Third, it is difficult to coordinate follow-on interactions and to rebuild interest once others have moved on.

You need to program yourself to react to the moment and reach out and start exploring to see what could be done with ambiguous opportunities. The most fruitful connections entail exploration with people who have complementary or adjacent expertise, cutting-edge technical insights, or unique market or client perspectives. Of all the things about networks that companies fail to tell their employees—and all the things that networking books fail to tell their readers—this is the biggest omission.

The lesson from this time horizon is to pause, for just a moment, and make sure you are not ignoring micro-moments that could define you. Success doesn't come from simply building a structurally diverse network where you are always interacting with people who are in other pockets of the organization. Rather, in the micro-moment, it comes in response to a request or idea and reaching out across network divides to people with unique expertise or perspectives who can help frame a better solution.

Leo, who we met earlier, is an example of reacting quickly and expansively to a short-horizon assignment. He knew he needed help right away with the product extension he was assigned to handle. The first person he went to was the original product's manager. This individual put him in touch with a data scientist and an engineer who could offer additional help with the product extension Leo was working on and help Leo fill his knowledge gaps.

To get others involved, Leo realized he needed to be clear about what he knew and enthusiastic about why others' work mattered to him. He was successful in bringing them on board: despite his youth and inexperience, he convened productive brainstorming sessions with them, tapping their knowledge and creativity. His roommate, too, was a good sounding board: he had a similar job in a different company and helped Leo think through the processes and the relationships.

These actions on Leo's part required going against the grain: "I kind of took a risk reaching out to some of the client side to get access to client feedback," he said. The solution he developed went well beyond what he was asked to do. And that success became the thing that put Leo on the top-talent list and led to future projects with far greater visibility than traditionally afforded someone of his tenure.

The Long Horizon: Seeding the Future

The long horizon is when you are seeding networks through exploration and creating scale through co-creation. Network-exploration investments in the long horizon are crucial because they enable you to see and solve problems differently than people who do not make these investments. These connections are what enable you to capitalize on the micro-moments (short horizon) and pivot well (medium horizon). But they are also the most challenging of all because the lack of any deadline tempts us to put them off or ignore them altogether.

As we've seen, the amazing thing about the most successful collaborators is that they don't put off or ignore these investments, no matter how busy things get. Instead, they are continually exploring and constantly co-creating.

Continually exploring

Successful collaborators create awareness of adjacent expertise through exploratory discussions. Engaging in exploratory interactions and cultivating network connections ahead of any specific need dramatically affects their capacity to spot opportunities. This practice also shapes their ability to frame more-encompassing and more-relevant problem and solution trajectories.

Deep knowledge of a network creates a wider aperture for seeing and shaping novel solutions. When confronted with a challenge or opportunity, people with a rich sense of the expertise and capabilities around them see possibilities largely because of who they know. High performers create this depth of awareness through intentional, exploratory discussions across silos.

Stories of career-defining successes consistently emphasized the importance of knowing expertise throughout the network. For example, consider a finance manager who worked for years with a client on restructuring the client's long-term strategy. Recalling conversations with colleagues in two other areas of the business, she envisioned a solution that led her to create a cross-unit team that developed and managed a new scope of work: "When you learn who knows what, in other parts of the organization, and cultivate those relationships, it broadens your view and can spark an idea when you are working on a project," she said. She proposed the idea, which resulted in a solution that merged several instruments to address the client's need. Without cross-unit relationships, this manager would have offered a routine, transactional service rather than a higher-margin solution that became a successful product line and a career-defining moment for her.

Good long-horizon collaborators make exploratory discussions with their networks routine. They embrace routines that systematically set up meetings to discuss how they could potentially work with others to achieve greater impact. They use these meetings to familiarize themselves with, and to spread awareness of, the interests and expertise residing in their networks. They take time to have off-task conversations, and they constantly ask questions that are outside the scope of any particular project.

In addition, they often hold forums that provide insight into their or their teams' work. In these forums, they engage in creative dialogues to help people envision how their capabilities could potentially address a problem or solution space.

You can do this too. When you do it, always situate the information about your capabilities within the context of others' needs. "We used to start with a stock presentation to try and get line units to see how to better come to us," one leader said. "It never really worked. Then one day a technical issue forced me off slides and to a discussion where I just had the people in the room tell me their top five problems. I put the problems on a flipchart, and we had an unbelievable dialogue on how we could help. The dialogue turned into a phenomenal collaboration with that group . . . It never would have happened if I was just presenting."

The good long-horizon collaborators' reputations for curiosity actually generate ideas. Knowing that the successful collaborators will be interested and open-minded, people come to them with all kinds of faint glimmers of unformed impressions, hypotheses, and hunches. In give-and-take in hallways, stairways, elevators, and pubs, these vague notions evolve into well-formed ideas. These are exhilarating experiences that both the high performers and their colleagues enjoy. The result is that the high performers are seen as "idea people," when in fact their main asset is their receptivity.

The point is that these long-term explorations are an essential part of the work of successful people in today's hyperconnected organizations. These interactions are not things to do when you have time. They are as essential as the work itself.

But you need to do them in a way that creates network efficiency. Successful people do this through early co-creation.

Constantly co-creating

Effective collaborators are *not* exclusively focused on how new colleagues in their networks can help them. Rather, their orientation and the ways they navigate discussions are around what could be done together. They are always thinking about constituents' needs. They understand that co-creation means co-ownership, and co-ownership brings forth others' time and energy.

They invest in learning the aspirations and talents of employees and colleagues across silos and boundaries. Then they co-create solutions, incorporating those aspirations and tapping those talents. They delegate in ways that create clarity and engagement, expressing trust by granting latitude.

This relationship foundation is critical in the short-term micro-moments and medium-term pivot points. You know this yourself. When you get an outreach from people who have just celebrated their own accomplishments or inquired into your expertise solely for their own needs, you are reluctant to help, at best. In contrast, help is often enthusiastically forthcoming when the successful collaborators ask, because they earlier interacted with others in ways that bred trust and engagement in mutual pursuits. For the successful people, this is not a game of indiscriminate networking but rather targeted investments that provide innovation, execution, and efficiency through connections.

When Abby was promoted to lead a newly formed practice area of a global professional-services firm, she made a well-planned effort to gain awareness of where types of expertise lay in the network. She held one-on-one meetings with managers and technical experts who would help establish the new practice area. She took time to understand what they currently did, their career histories, and the type of work they were most interested in. She asked them who else was doing interesting work or might have skills or knowledge related to what they were doing; then she followed up to build ties into other functions, levels, and locations. She arranged regular one-on-one meetings with the other practice leaders, her boss, and other vice presidents, establishing trust and rapport with senior leadership.

Even as she became immersed in business development and client delivery, Abby routinely had coffee or lunch to meet newcomers or stay connected with colleagues across the organization. "You have to map out these meetings or check-ins every week, even when you think you don't have time," she said. "It's an essential part of the job. It's the only way you have access to expertise or can connect the dots to help you make decisions."

Before discussing the nuts and bolts of an idea, the high performers ensure that everyone fully understands the work's reason for being. What is the ultimate purpose of the idea? How does it help everyone meet mutually beneficial goals? They invite people to validate the importance of the work. By doing this, the high performers consistently achieve greater engagement from their employees and colleagues.

They also take the broadest possible view of the concept of "why." They think about why the work matters to the company as a whole; why it matters to the world; why it matters to their own careers; why they will feel great about it—or not—after all is said and done.

About a year into her new role, Abby saw an opportunity to pursue a complex project that was beyond the scope of her group. Rather than dismissing it as too ambitious, she envisioned a strategic capability that combined expertise across three practice areas.

From her many exploratory conversations, she remembered a project in the same sector. She knew of others in the firm who might be willing to collaborate, and she was aware of teams that had related technical skills. She also knew an ambitious project manager who was seeking a bigger, high-profile opportunity.

It was this awareness of capacity in the network that prompted Abby to think deeply about what was possible—an investment that resulted in an innovative proposal, a new way to service large clients, and a huge win for Abby and her organization.

But Who Has the Time?

OK, I know what you're thinking: you're much too busy to do all this network development. Let me remind you that the people I studied didn't have huge networks of dozens of people, nor did they spend hours at networking events. They had from a half dozen to two dozen choice, well-placed network ties that were mutually rewarding. Of course, they knew and could turn to a much larger population, but their core network typically fell into this range.

Let's break this down to see the actual time commitments. A typical high performer we studied characterized the time investment like this:

- *Short-horizon micro-moments.* Two to four hours a month. Most ideas don't go anywhere, but a few matter substantially. (Even the ideas that don't go anywhere end up seeding relationships.)

- *Medium-horizon network investments around execution.* Eight to twelve hours a month across all categories, depending on the point in the project life cycle.

- *Long-horizon exploration investments.* Six to eight hours a month.

Obviously these numbers vary by role, level, and, to some degree, personality. But let's say for a typical person, an average is somewhere between sixteen to twenty-four hours a month in these activities. This is not a ridiculous amount in the context of the enormous payoff. But it does point to the critical role of freeing time to make these investments (see chapters 3–5).

This is not the kind networking where you put an hour or two a week into phone calls. This is truly a different way of driving innovation and execution in an interconnected world. However, efficient collaborators get back more than enough time for these interactions. And the true payoff is a much higher likelihood of staying on the high-performer path and engaging in spheres of life that fuel our well-being.

What you need to keep in mind is the efficiency in work that tends to accrue for these people. Opportunities flow *to* people who engage in this way due to their reputations. And those who connect in the way I am describing across the time horizons experience less friction in trying to get plans through later. What can take a less connected colleague days if not weeks of bullet-proofing an idea becomes one meeting with high energy and engagement for these successful women and men.

And as your reputation builds, your future work meets less friction.

. . .

I have heard people complain time and again that they'll never succeed at developing their networks because they're not comfortable hobnobbing with crowds, or they're not especially "social," or they're not "political."

But the most-effective collaborators showed me that their success in investing in network resources had nothing to do with any of that. They didn't amass vast networks. Many of them weren't especially social. And none of them were magically connected politically. They succeeded because they were selective about the makeup of their networks, and they focused on producing outcomes of greater value for themselves and others.

They also showed me the power of reputation in pulling people, ideas, and opportunities toward themselves. That is the topic of the next chapter.

7

Energizing Connections

Can you identify a time when you were *energized* at work? In other words, was there a time when you gave more effort than you would have expected to, in work that you wouldn't have thought was particularly exciting, because someone infused the task with energy and spurred your enthusiasm?

Maybe a client visit you had been dreading turned into an inspiring interaction that led to great things. Or maybe you took on a sidetrack assignment to manage a team that was doing something mundane, yet the experience proved to be a milestone in your career. Or maybe you completed training in something seemingly dull, but the topic really came alive, and the next thing you knew you were the resident expert on it.

Maybe it wasn't a particular event or task but rather a stretch of time when, overall, you felt energized—a time when you frequently woke up with a feeling of eagerness and showed up in your work fully engaged. Can you remember *why* you felt this way? What was happening? Can you sort out how much of the experience was about the nature of the work itself versus the ways you were collaborating with people around the work?

If you think about it, chances are it was less about the work and more about the interactions. The client visit became inspiring because your counterpart was so passionate and engaged. What you thought was going to be a mundane piece of work became a memorable experience because the team commitment and chemistry were so great. The topic of that training came alive because there was something special about the instructor or ways that colleagues in the program envisioned possible applications.

When I ask these questions, it's always a joy to see people light up and to hear what made the difference for them during these moments or stretches of time. They talk about experiences such as latching onto a boss's belief in inspiring goals, or of being motivated by a culture of co-creation, or by a sense of ownership, or by personal connections with teammates—or even by a colleague's offbeat sense of humor. All of these are sources of energy. (See the sidebar "Discovering Energy.")

People sometimes think this topic is soft, too metaphysical or froofy, but it's not. Energy is a down-to-earth, workaday thing. Energy is built through behaviors that people can learn. And it's massively important for success today.

Consider Pauline, a corporate executive whose leadership was being put to the test.

Quiet but Energizing

Pauline was director of sustainability for the chocolate business of her global food company. Sustainability had become a critical factor in maintaining and increasing profit, but for many years the corporation had allowed each business unit to establish its own approach to it. Pauline's assignment from the CEO was to create uniform policies and standards for the whole company—a big change that would potentially put her in conflict with the business-unit leaders.

Given her position, Pauline might have been expected to start issuing orders from on high, but that's not how she approached the project.

Discovering Energy

One day I was walking down the hall in the Boston office of a Connected Commons member, a global consulting firm, and the head partner stopped dead in front of me. I thought I was in his path, so I tried to move aside, but he matched my step, which I guess was his particular way of saying, "Let's talk."

I looked up and he looked down, and he said, "Rob, we're all smart here. We get really good talent."

There was a weird, uncomfortable silence, like *What am I supposed to say?* I finally said, "Yes, you're all very smart and talented."

And they are. The firm is full of amazing people—people who are not just smart but have depth of perspective and worldview.

The reason for his comment about everyone being smart was that he had been wondering why some people in the firm were so much more successful than others. The conventional wisdom in the consulting world at the time was that one of the main keys was pure, raw intelligence: in order to be more successful than everyone else, it was assumed, you had to be that much smarter. The head partner rejected the conventional wisdom.

"I don't think what distinguishes our high performers is a couple of points of IQ," he said. "I don't think it's somebody who's marginally smarter who's winning this game."

"So what is it?" I asked.

"They get the partners engaged in what they're up to, their peers help them out, their teams give greater effort, and the client wants to buy more."

Through network mapping, analysis, and interviews, I learned what the head partner was talking about. It was *energy.*

Instead she relied on relationships in her network that she had been building for years with the business-unit leaders. "She often came here and spent time with us to understand the details of our business and learn about everyone's interests and aspirations," one business-unit leader said. Pauline spoke quietly and wasn't a flashy presenter or the center of attention—you could easily lose her in a crowd. But she was reflective and fully present in her interactions.

"We looked forward to her visits," the unit leader said. "She was simpatico. And she could be very funny in her own way—we loved being with her. Also, it was obvious that she cared deeply. She was a great help; somehow we were always more able to come up with creative solutions when she asked us her pointed questions. She was generous about offering corporate resources, and she always followed through. How many people do that these days?"

Having established these relationships, Pauline was in a good position to go to the business units and make the case for unifying the approach to sustainability. Her trusted long-time deputy, whom she brought along, delivered crisp, compelling presentations detailing how worldwide overproduction had suppressed chocolate prices, put intense pressure on margins, and weakened sustainability initiatives. He showed that a unified approach would bring down costs and enable the company to be more proactive about reducing child labor and about improving agricultural practices.

He wrapped up with an inspiring vision: "In challenging times, our products give a vital lift to people all over the world, from small children to powerful leaders," he said in a talk that Pauline had helped him write. "We are in the business of helping people find joy. But we must do more than this. We have a moral imperative to make our entire business more sustainable."

The business-unit leaders were quick to respond. One of them reminded Pauline that a past quality issue with the parent company's processing plant was the reason some of them had started buying cocoa butter from outside suppliers with questionable sustainability practices. But he said he was willing to go back to in-house supplies, which were produced in accordance with corporate policies, if Pauline could guarantee a certain quality level. He challenged the leaders of the other business units to make the same pledge, and they agreed.

Pauline and her deputy smiled at each other. It happened that Pauline had recently replaced the head of that Pennsylvania plant with a recognized master in the field whom she had serendipitously bumped into at a conference. The new manager was now settling into the job, and Pauline felt confident that he could achieve the quality turnaround that the business units demanded.

By the time Pauline and her deputy returned to headquarters, they had made significant headway on the project.

Following the Energizers' Playbook

People usually assume that in order to be an energizer, you have to be outgoing or charismatic. But that's wrong: neither extroversion nor charisma create energizers in and of themselves. Really strong energizers are just as likely to be understated, introverted, or low-key, like Pauline. You can be fully engaged and have a powerful impact without being a talker or demanding everyone's attention. Conversely, we have all known highly charismatic and outgoing people who don't create energy at all.

Organizations are often surprised to learn who their energizers are. When a colleague of mine did an analysis for the Broad Institute of MIT and Harvard, a biomedical research organization, the results were unexpected, said Kate O'Brien, the Broad's director of people insights. Many of the scientists who turned out to be energizers were low-profile employees. They weren't research stars, but they were connectors—they were the Kevin Bacons in the organization, touching many different areas. "They're really essential people," she said. "Should they decide to go somewhere else, we would start to feel enthusiasm and mission-focused collaboration falling off in the culture." (See the Coaching Break, "Six Energy-Building Behaviors.")

Six Energy-Building Behaviors
ARE YOU LETTING ANY OF THESE SLIP?

I assume that you engage in all six of these energy-generating behaviors whenever possible. The real question is: When and why do you let them slip? Ask yourself: Which one or two of these behaviors do I neglect when I am under stress or pressure? Once you have identified them, try to be more systematic about exhibiting these behaviors.

1. In meetings and one-on-one conversations, **I engage others in realistic possibilities** that capture their imaginations and hearts.

   Why this matters. Stretch goals are exciting, but they need to be realistic in order to be embraced as feasible, without fear that they will generate an unreasonable workload.

   What you can do. In conversations, emphasize not only the value of an idea but also its achievability.

2. **I am typically fully engaged** in meetings and one-on-one conversations, and I show my interest in others and their ideas.

   Why this matters. People need to know that you think they and their ideas are valuable.

   What you can do. Lean in, adopt an open stance, maintain eye contact, smile, nod, stay focused, listen actively, keep mental track of the conversation, use an engaging voice, ignore your ringing phone, and don't get distracted thinking about what you're going to say next.

3. **I create room for others** to be meaningful contributors to conversations and make sure they see how their efforts become part of an evolving plan.

Why this matters. Enthusiasm for a project increases if people believe that their efforts can have real impact.

What you can do. Be humble. Acknowledge others' ideas and perspectives. Create opportunities for them to participate in problem solving and feedback. Build on their ideas. Be appreciative. Be judicious in applying your own expertise. Don't take yourself or your ideas too seriously.

4. When I disagree with someone's plan or a course of action, I **focus on the issue at hand and not the individual.**

   Why this matters. Focusing on the individual shuts down interest and progress.

   What you can do. When you criticize, stay centered on the idea, not the person. And, most importantly, offer your own thinking for exploration.

5. **I use humor**, often at my own expense, to lighten tense moments or remove status or politics from interactions.

   Why this matters. Humor, especially the self-deprecating kind, can change the mood, reenergize people, remove tension, counteract unnecessary hierarchy in a group, encourage others to be authentic, and enable people to take risks with their ideas.

   What you can do. Look for opportunities to make light of yourself or a "common enemy," such as a competitor. Don't joke too much—be judicious. And don't take risks joking at others' expense unless you are sure of their reaction.

6. **I maintain an effective balance** between pushing toward a goal and welcoming new ideas that can improve the project or the process for reaching the goal.

(continued)

> **Why this matters.** People stay engaged when they are able to adjust the plan to make it better. Ideas from the group allow for progress in unexpected directions.
>
> **What you can do.** Be open and flexible about how to achieve goals. Ask for others' opinions and reactions. But stay focused on solutions and make sure people leave meetings knowing what steps to take.

To look at Pauline, you would never have said she projected a "star" persona. Yet she was a classic energizer, following the playbook to a T. For one thing, she engaged people in realistic possibilities that captured their imaginations and hearts. Sourcing cocoa butter from the company's own processing plant was a realistic option, and she and her deputy presented it as both a rational and an emotional win. Moreover, she was a frequent user of humor—often at her own expense—to lighten tense moments or remove unnecessary status or politics from interactions. She also maintained an effective balance between pushing toward a goal and welcoming new ideas. Witness how the solution was co-created with the business-unit leaders.

Energizers' Performance Secret: Pull

Should you strive to be an energizer? Yes. Energizers are three to four times as likely as nonenergizers to achieve top performance ratings and get promoted, and they are two to three times as likely to successfully manage their career transitions. In fact, I have found that, statistically, being an energizer is the biggest predictor of individuals' long-term success and well-being. Having a diverse network and making good use of it, which we explored in the previous chapter, is a big predictor of success too, but if you're an energizer on top of that, it's *four times* the predictor of high performance that network diversity alone is.

Think about this surprising finding for a minute. The biggest predictor of success isn't network size, charisma, sociability, a big vocabulary, or a winning smile. It's whether or not you're an energizer. It's whether people tend to walk away from you feeling more enthused, a little bit more excited about what you are up to (which is critical if they are your leaders or key stakeholders) and what they are up to (which is critical if they are your peers or people who report to you).

The reason energizers win is what I call *pull*. This is not "pull" in the sense of clout; it's the ability to draw talent, ideas, and opportunities to you. If you have this quality, you are better than others at attracting and retaining great people. You get greater creativity out of the individuals around you. People are more willing to help you. You get better support for your ideas and projects. And you are better at making serendipity happen for you.

Pull was the key to Pauline's success. Think about her deputy, Wilmer, known as Willy, who delivered the sustainability presentations. He was crucial to her, and he was unique. No other executive in the company had someone like Willy.

Because Pauline was an energizer, Willy was drawn to her. He wanted to work with her. Pauline reciprocated. From the time Willy came on board in the accounting department, she sought to understand not only his strengths and weaknesses, but also what he wanted to do and where he wanted to go in the company. She appreciated his alacrity in getting things done and his phenomenal attention to detail but sensed his discomfort with being in positions of independent authority. Over time, she came to see that he really aspired to become a top-notch number two, an aide-de-camp. Such a position didn't exist, so she created it for him.

Willy and Pauline complemented each other; where Pauline faltered, as in public speaking, Willy excelled. They were better as a pair than either of them had been individually.

And then there was the new head of the plant Pauline had hired. True, she had randomly bumped into him at a conference, but then pull took over. This individual recognized Pauline's energizing qualities and spent quite a bit of time with her at the conference. He was receptive as she recruited him for months afterward.

OK, you may be saying at this point, *I get that there's such a thing as energy, and that the performance advantages of energizers are all about pull. But these ideas are so abstract. How do I generate pull myself?*

One manager pointed out to me that when a new project comes along—a project that is someone else's idea—his team's first reaction is to groan. "We almost never get excited about someone else's ideas," he said. "Typically, after the presentation, we'll get together and commiserate. Our first impulse is to talk about how this is going to add to our workload and how we're all going to end up getting screwed." These kinds of apprehensions about new projects are common and understandable.

But, the manager told me, the team reacts very differently if it sees a valuable purpose in the work and if the idea comes from someone the team trusts. "Only in the context of purpose and trust do we let go of our reservations," the manager said.

Purpose and trust are the foundations of creating energy and pull in networks.

Create Pull with Purpose

People tend to assume that a sense of purpose comes with an organization's mission, that in order to feel a strong sense of purpose, you need to work for a company that is striving to find a cure for a dreaded disease, for example. And yes, company mission can be an important ingredient. Pauline worked with Willy to make sure that he instilled in the business units a clear sense that their work was helping people, emphasizing that the company was about enabling people to find joy. Other organizations center the "why" on meeting a mission or delivering financial results.

FIGURE 7-1

Organizational network analysis: Creating a sense of purpose at an investment bank

The dots represent individuals in a group, with dark dots showing the top leaders. Lines reflect who felt a sense of purpose in their interactions with others. Throughout the entire network of close to four thousand, the top quartile of leaders created a sense of purpose for almost sixteen other people on average. The bottom quartile did not do that for even one person (again, on average).

While both groups of leaders were working hard, it was the top quartile that enjoyed benefits of scale: people gave more to their work, were more innovative in solutions and ideas, and stayed longer.

But less well appreciated is the importance of people in instilling purpose. You can actually map purpose in organizations. It can be done with organizational network analysis (ONA), a term that covers a range of tools from a number of vendors depicting the relationships within a given group.[1] ONA can identify people who occupy a range of network roles, including collaboration builders, connectors, experts, brokers, energizers, de-energizers, and fearmongers. (See figure 7-1.)

For example, when we asked the top six hundred leaders of an investment bank, "Who among you inspires a greater sense of purpose in your work after an interaction?" we could then use ONA to see how people connected. It showed us that at this bank, the top quartile of leaders created a sense of purpose for nearly sixteen other people, on average. The bottom quartile, in stark contrast, managed to generate a sense of purpose for less than one person.

It's no surprise that the top quartile attracted higher performers and retained them longer. In essence, they obtained scale from their networks by enabling others to feel a sense of purpose in their work.

ONA suggests that interpersonal collaborations account for as much as half of employees' sense of purpose. We also analyzed a retail chain. Although the company was essentially a sales platform—not the kind of organization that people are typically drawn to as a beacon of purpose—among the employees there existed a clear sense of purpose.

The leaders of the retailer diffuse ownership so that employees have a sense of a cooperative undertaking—their purpose is to help one another achieve. They invest in learning the backgrounds, interests, and aspirations of people in order to structure work to align with others' career aspirations.

Purpose gives people a reason to commit greater effort. That's why instilling a sense of purpose in others gives you greater pull; it motivates people to gravitate toward you and causes a flow of ideas and opportunities to come your way. Pull is a key part of being an energizer and of sparking people to bring their best in the moment. Through hundreds of interviews, my colleagues and I have identified eleven purpose-building behaviors that can be learned and applied. (See the Coaching Break, "Eleven Purpose-Building Behaviors.")

Create Pull with Trust

The degree to which we engage with others in ways that rapidly create trust in us is a blind spot for most of us. Once, I was leading a conversation with roughly two hundred people, all of whom had decks of cards in front of them. The cards focused on behaviors that foster trust, purpose, and energy in interactions. I asked the participants to create three stacks of these cards—one stack of the trust behaviors, one of

Eleven Purpose-Building Behaviors

People often assume that a sense of purpose is always tied to a company's mission, but interpersonal collaborations account for as much as half of employees' sense of purpose. In the list, identify one or at most two behaviors that, if you focused on more, would generate a greater sense of purpose in those around you.

1. I help people clarify and pursue meaningful career objectives.

2. I help structure work to align with others' career aspirations.

3. I establish the importance of work (the "why") before the tactics for accomplishing it (the "what" or the "how").

4. I co-create solutions and diffuse ownership early.

5. I encourage people to be attuned to and synchronized with the demands their colleagues face.

6. I show appreciation for others' work.

7. I encourage fun in work.

8. I reframe negative interactions to focus on work worth doing.

9. I encourage people to find purpose by helping others.

10. I coach people to collaborate at a pace and in cycles that allow them to work at their best.

11. I encourage people to find purpose in their work through networks inside and outside the organization.

the purpose behaviors, and one of the energy behaviors—and then to select one card from whichever stack represented the area where they felt they most needed improvement. To my amazement, nearly all of them pulled cards from either the purpose or the energy stack. Just one person took a card from the trust stack.

The pattern repeated in other sessions, suggesting that the vast majority of us don't feel we need to work on trust, or at least that building trust is not a priority for us. We trust ourselves to act in ways that we believe are right, and we simply assume that others will have the same trust in us. If we have a one-to-one meeting scheduled at 2 p.m., we trust ourselves to show up on time, and we assume that the other person will trust us equally, because we see ourselves as inherently trustworthy. It can be shocking to hear a colleague say that she came late to a meeting because she assumed that *we* wouldn't be on time. We don't think enough about whether our behaviors are actually trustworthy—whether our behaviors truly inspire others to trust us as we so readily trust ourselves.

Trust is a critical foundation for pull and for energy. The refreshingly candid manager who was quoted earlier in this chapter put it well: "We almost never get excited about someone else's ideas" unless the ideas are presented in the context of purpose and trust. People just don't get energized by ideas that are presented outside of a trusting relationship. If there's a trust gap, people shy away from engaging with new ideas, no matter how elegantly they are presented.

The gap might have to do with *benevolence-based trust*, meaning that the person doubts we have her interests in mind (briefly discussed in chapter 2). Or the hesitation might have to do with *competence-based trust*, meaning that she senses that our project will ultimately fail because we don't really know what we're talking about. Or it might be a lack of *integrity-based trust*, which is based on the sense that we may not do what we say we're going to do.

An individual who feels a lack of benevolence-based trust in her dealings with us will resist getting energized by our idea, because she doesn't want to be a pawn in our game of personal strategy. If she feels a lack of competence-based trust, she will start looking for escape routes to avoid getting stuck with a project that she feels is likely to crash. If she feels a lack of integrity-based trust, then she will automatically go on defense to avoid getting buried under extra work.

In chapter 6, we saw that in order to innovate successfully, we need to capitalize rapidly on short-term opportunities while sculpting future possibilities through specific kinds of network initiation and development. In essence, we need to make a leap of faith, letting go of control, embracing ambiguity, and reaching out early to our networks. These kinds of network interactions, which generate significant exchanges of knowledge, can only take place in a context of well-developed trust. My research shows that benevolence-based and competence-based trust are critical to the success of knowledge exchange, particularly when the knowledge is tacit or the people exchanging information are new to the problem space, as is often the case in early-stage problem-solving.[2]

Building trust comes from engaging in behaviors that quickly enable others to trust you, which provides a critical foundation for energy. In most cases, the behaviors that build trust are small and easy. An executive who is a turnaround specialist told me that the first thing he does on joining a new organization is to initiate a discussion about people's backgrounds and values and use that discussion to talk candidly about himself—a classic "soft and fuzzy" activity designed to put people at ease.

I saw the logic of this when I met him: He was a behemoth who had been an Olympic wrestler. He looked as though he could crush a brick. He knows how people react when they see him. "There are so many ways that people who don't know me can infer poor intent," he said with characteristic understatement. "And they can spread those inferences to others in interactions I don't even see or hear about. So I have found that if I get out in front of this and give people a sense of who I am, how I am making decisions, where I am coming from, a lot of this misunderstanding never happens."

Through the action of initiating a discussion, he intentionally creates benevolence-based trust. Similarly, simple behaviors can help build competence-based trust—for example, when you present a new-product idea, show instances of where analogous things have been successfully tried. And there are a million ways you can build integrity-based trust, such as by following through on all of your commitments, no matter how seemingly trivial.

Long before she needed to move the business units toward a new way of doing things, Pauline had established all three kinds of trust. For example, she offered the units her time, insights, and guidance, and provided resources where needed, all without expecting a quid pro quo, and she frequently connected with people off task, seeking to understand their backgrounds, interests, and aspirations. She made a new hire to improve the quality output of the company's plant, demonstrating her competency. And as the business-unit leader pointed out, "she always followed through"—she demonstrated integrity by making good on her commitments.

My colleagues and I have identified ten trust-building behaviors that can be learned and applied. (See the Coaching Break, "Ten Trust-Building Behaviors.")

The Outsized Impact of De-Energizers

Sadly, in the organizations I have studied, nonenergizers greatly outnumbered energizers. On the network map that I created for the consulting firm described in the sidebar "Discovering Energy," as you progressed toward the edge, you could see the people who were less connected and less energizing. Way out on the fringe of the map, I found one partner who had very few connections and energized nobody.

There are also *de-energizers* who are the opposite of Pauline. De-energizers see obstacles or constraints at all turns, and they articulate flaws in plans before you can fully explain the plans. Rather than limiting themselves to criticizing ideas, they place blame on others and disagree personally. They're like Winnie-the-Pooh's friend Eeyore, sapping energy just by their presence. Even a small number of these people can have a deadening effect on a group. Statistically, in our models pre-

COACHING BREAK

Ten Trust-Building Behaviors

Instead of asking yourself how trustworthy you are, focus on behaviors: Do you engage in behaviors that rapidly create a foundation of trust? In the list, identify one or at most two behaviors that would create greater trust around you if you engaged in them more thoughtfully.

1. I make others want to turn to me for transparent, credible expertise.

2. I acknowledge areas in which I am not an expert.

3. I create rich interactions at key points in projects.

4. I encourage others to critique and improve my ideas.

5. I offer time, resources, information, referrals, insights, and other assistance before I ask for help and without expectation of benefit.

6. I connect with people off task, seeking to understand their backgrounds, interests, and aspirations.

7. I am consistent in communicating my values and priorities.

8. I do what I say I am going to do and follow through on commitments I make to people.

9. I am committed to principles and goals that are larger than my own self-interest.

10. I keep confidential or revealing information to myself.

dicting performance, the de-energizers tend to have twice the negative impact that the energizers have on a positive front.

De-energizers can also be found in relationships and groups outside of work. One leader described a de-energizer in her cycling group: "Three or four of us would go cycling after work together, and while the exercise was great, it was almost counterproductive, because there was one woman who was stressing me out. She was constantly going on about how she hated her job, and her husband was so awful, and everything. In the end, I stopped cycling with them, and other people dropped out of the group for the same reason."

. . .

One of the most pernicious effects of collaboration overload is that it undermines our capacity and motivation to be energizers. I used to assume that de-energizers were born, not made, that they were placed on this earth to make life unbearable for the rest of us. But a few years back, a grad student examined our longitudinal data and found that most people who were identified as de-energizers had not started out that way. Many of them had started out as energizers, but something slipped along the way.

In other words, we are all potential de-energizers. We might have started out as energizers, and we might still have the best intentions, but collaboration overload has turned us into the people we never wanted to be. One of the key things that slips if we don't combat overload is ways of interacting that energize others. If we are overloaded, we come into interactions too focused on what *we* need to get done. We don't take time to acknowledge others' past efforts. We focus on the "what" and miss the importance of discussing the "why" to ensure that the work has purpose and meaning, and that we operate in a context of trust.

The behaviors underlying trust, purpose, and energy are not difficult to implement, but they do require us to be intentional. Intentionality is the crux of the next chapter, which pulls together everything we have seen in this book about overload, networks, and energy to create a path toward the ultimate goal: well-being.

8

Thriving in a Connected World

"Out of nowhere, I had a business trip canceled and free time on my hands. I went home on a beautiful summer day, and as I pulled into my driveway, I realized my family was scattered doing their things and that I had no friends to reach out to or hobbies that I had once loved. I sat in the car for more than an hour thinking about how I had gotten to that point."

This comment, from a well-regarded software executive, reflects a pattern I have heard in hundreds of interviews of successful executives. Leaving college with a range of interests and friends, they choose a career that optimizes money, status, and maybe a sense of impact. Work ramps up quickly to twelve-plus-hour days. The combination of work, commuting, and travel results in exercise—especially in groups—declining and social worlds narrowing to work and select friends. Soon they find themselves in an echo chamber where work defines their entire existence for years. They fall out of the last of the groups and activities that had helped them cope, and if these were skill-related like music, tennis, or even running with a club, it becomes almost impossible to catch up. If they are lucky, they wake up in an epiphany moment like my Silicon Valley friend.

When I think of well-being, I don't mean a fleeting feeling of happiness. Rather, well-being is an individual's sense of satisfaction with their life as a whole, the feeling that "life is good." A person with high well-being has inner contentment, an enduring sense of fulfillment, and a view that life is heading in a good direction. Unfortunately for many, well-being is elusive. People today feel more under the gun than ever, pressured by endless collaborative demands, long hours, sleep deprivation, and always-on technology. According to the Gallup-Sharecare Well-Being Index, the United States has experienced a two-year decline in well-being, ending at an all-time low in what Gallup's research director calls "an unprecedented decline in well-being nationally."[1]

Behind the decline, Gallup finds a consistent erosion in the elements of social well-being, defined as having supportive relationships and love in your life, and career well-being, or liking what you do and feeling motivated toward your goals. Of course, this idea of relationships being central to well-being is not new. Every model on well-being or happiness has relationships as a core component for people who are thriving. But the models don't tell you how to initiate or sustain the right kinds of connections. They don't tell you what to do if you have fallen out of groups and lost these relationships. And they certainly don't speak to the almost-invisible ways that stress gets created through connections today.

I am not a psychologist or therapist. But I have interviewed enough people about their well-being, or the lack of it, to see strong patterns emerge. Throughout my interviews, people who told a positive life story almost always described authentic connections in two, three, or four groups outside of work: athletic pursuits, volunteer work, civic or religious communities, book or dinner clubs, and so on. Ideally, one of the groups supports physical health—through nutrition and/or exercise norms. And one or two more add dimensionality on intellectual, spiritual, social, or civic fronts. These groups cohere around some common interest or history and help us connect with people from a wide range of life experiences.

The interactions with these people broaden our identity and how we look at our lives. They help us shrug off old identities and remake ourselves into a new and larger person. They shape who we are and how we look at the world. And, perhaps most importantly today, they give us courage to pursue life a little more on our terms and a little less in service of the always-on work demands.

In contrast, when I talked to people who were on their second or sometimes third marriages, physically unhealthy to a point of crisis, or with children who merely tolerated them, I would almost always find that these people had allowed life to become unidimensional. Work success had come to dominate these people's definition of life success and had slowly taken them out of all groups and activities not associated with this trajectory. Often this felt great: like they were doing critically important things, with other people who were their friends, and they were taking care of their families. This all made sense, right up until a stark awakening. As one highly successful female software executive told me, "My mother battled cancer and passed away after seven very difficult months . . . No one from a company I had given eight hard years of my life to showed up at the funeral."

Loss of physical vitality and dimensionality in life makes us susceptible in today's highly connected world. When all of our relational investments lie in work, we are often pulled into being someone we don't want to be and experience the vagaries of corporate life too deeply.

A seductive way of dealing with the unending demands of work life today is to justify the sacrifices as being for the benefit of our families. And too often the people I spoke with—at some point in their lives—took this one step too far: purchasing a home that was an improvement for their families or moving into a school district that they felt was critical for their children's success.

Of course, it is not that family—close or extended—is a bad choice. Family is a critical anchor for most of us. But when it becomes all you have, and you justify the sacrifices for family alone, it leads to vulnerability. This is not materialism in the sense that we often think. People were not defining success exclusively through possessions like a new car or a fancy watch. More insidiously, a social-comparison process— what it means to be a good provider or caregiver—defined what many conventionally successful people thought they needed and pulled them out of the groups and meaningful relationships that provided a sense of well-being.

If this resonates with you, the question is how to emerge from the echo chamber—or, better yet, how to avoid entering it. Where do you start?

My research suggests three important, interconnected strategies:

- *Maintain physical health with others.* Those who are all in on their careers—in other words, those for whom work is not a side gig or hobby—typically experience a downward spiral in physical health starting between the ages of thirty-five and forty. As demands from work and home intensify, they often fall out of groups and activities that help them maintain their health. This is problematic, as exercise in particular is one of the most-effective ways to combat the insidious effects of stress as well as ensure that we bring vitality and energy to our work and life. The people I found who were more successful in persisting in a more health-oriented lifestyle almost always embedded these activities in a set of connections that both kept them accountable and formed meaningful, authentic relationships that in turn shaped who they were as people.

- *Shield from the negative by managing micro-stressors intentionally.* Stress is the number-one driver of poor health. We all experience relationally driven stress at a volume, velocity, and intensity that dramatically affects our well-being. These are all seemingly small moments that in reality sit with us for hours or days and drive a more negative impact on our well-being than we realize. Too often, we allow these micro-stressors to invisibly pile up in our lives and simply try to fight through each day, develop coping mechanisms, or hope that things will get better just over the horizon. Successful people, in contrast, are more proactive. They routinely identify and act to minimize the impact of systemic micro-stressors.

- *Add dimensionality to life through interactions that generate purpose and meaning.* It has become popular to think of
  purpose and meaning as being derived from the work we do.
  But in reality, 50 percent or more of our sense of purpose and
  meaning comes from our interactions with other people, both
  inside and outside of work. The goal should be to make subtle
  shifts to activities that pull you into social spheres that yield a
  sense of purpose for you. Surprisingly, identifying and implementing just a few slight shifts can have a significant impact
  on well-being.

These seemingly small actions have a tremendous impact in distinguishing those who thrive in their careers and lives. Let's explore each
in a little more depth.

Maintain Physical Health with Others

Physical health plays a unique role in well-being. How we feel about
our health is a strong predictor of how we feel about our lives. Un-
derstandably, feeling physically well gives us the energy and capability
to show up at work more vibrantly, to engage others in our efforts, to
take steps toward greater well-being, and to respond to challenges in
a more positive way. Research consistently shows that people who have
satisfying relationships with family, friends, and community have fewer
health problems, lower levels of anxiety and depression, and live longer.
Positive connections have been related to lower blood pressure, better
immune response, and a healthier inflammatory process, with implications for reduced risk of diseases such as cardiovascular disease, stroke,
and cancer. In contrast, social isolation has been found to be "on a par
with high blood pressure, obesity, lack of exercise, or smoking as a risk
factor for illness and early death."[2] One theory even treats social isolation, conflict, or lack of support as chronically stressful conditions to
which our bodies respond by aging more rapidly.

Connections with others drive health behaviors through setting norms. Many health-related outcomes move through social networks in a process called "social contagion." For example, a landmark study of 4,700 people over twenty years found that an individual's chance of becoming obese increased by 57 percent if that individual had a friend who became obese in a given time period. Mental-health outcomes have also been found to be "contagious": the odds that a person will become depressed increase by 118 percent if a friend is depressed, and the likelihood of a person being happy increases 63 percent if a nearby friend becomes happy.[3]

Interestingly, in the obesity study, it was not going to fast-food restaurants or cooking high-fat meals together that primarily drove the contagion; increasing geographic distance among people did not diminish the effect. Instead, the key driver was a change in people's norms about the acceptability of being overweight. With obesity considered normative, the barriers to overeating and sedentary behavior were lowered. The norms established by others in the workplace can also shape our behavior in ways that affect physical and mental well-being. Expectations for long workdays and 24-7 accessibility have become common in many workplaces—sometimes by direct need, but more often by the habits and culture around us. They signal to us that long hours mean commitment and loyalty; indicate toughness, strength, and competitiveness; and mark how indispensable we are.

How do we, as individuals, combat what is going on around us? What can we learn from people who adopt and persist in healthier lifestyles despite these pressures? Close to a decade ago, one of the world's most respected health-insurance organizations came to me with this question. The company's chief learning officer at the time said, "We love the research on networks of high performers. But we would also like to understand the connectivity strategies of physically healthy people. In other words, if people decide to change their health, are there certain kinds of network connections that increase their odds of success over time?"

This thoughtful question ultimately inspired a range of quantitative studies over the years to relate people's personal networks to measures of physical health—days absent, body mass index (BMI), cholesterol levels, blood pressure, and self-reported measures of health.

Two important ideas emerged from this work.

First, we could systematically see that people who decided to adopt a more health-conscious lifestyle, and were able to persist in it, enjoyed unique benefits from positive connections around them. In particular, they were more likely to be surrounded by people who influenced their nutrition decisions, their physical activity, and their sense that taking care of themselves was worth doing. In all of the studies we have done, this is the one area where introverts face a systematic disadvantage.

Second—and the real eye-opener—was the disproportionate health impact of negative ties. These connections take two primary forms: people who create stress, and people who enable unhealthy behaviors. The latter group includes people you might go to the gym with but then accompany to a high-carbohydrate meal or drinks that reverse all the positive impact and more. In fact, one study showed that some people needed up to 7.2 positive ties to outweigh the effects of one negative tie.

So, clearly, a focus on ameliorating the negative connections is critical. We just have to find these people and banish them from our lives, right?

Not so fast, it turns out. In all of these studies, when we would prompt people to indicate the most-positive relational influences on their health, we would typically hear some variant of significant other, children, friends, and extended family. Then we would prompt these same people to identify the individuals with the greatest *negative* impact on their health—the stress creators and enablers. And we often got an almost identical list—significant other, children, friends, and family. So the problem wasn't so much the specific people as the intermingling of negative and positive health-oriented behaviors in these relationships. The trick was not to banish the negative influencer but to alter the behaviors within the relationships.

Intervening in these connections was critical to success because they enabled a net negative cycle that had to be broken in order for people to move toward a positive trajectory. Our quantitative network models showed that:

1. Negative self-perception increased as people became less healthy; this led to

2. a greater propensity toward isolation (for introverts) or negative health ties, which in turn led to

3. a tendency toward activities that hurt physical health through decreased exercise or poorer eating (in particular, fast food), which in turn led to

4. increased BMI, which, you guessed it, was statistically associated with the factor that started this cycle, increased negative self-perception.

No wonder our New Year's resolutions rarely make it to January 15. And no wonder so many corporate HR executives bemoan the fact that people do not take advantage of benefits that could promote healthy living. Helping people become healthy is not about getting them to make a few specific isolated decisions; instead it is about changing a social ecosystem. Let's look more deeply at stories of success.

Shifting life stories through connections

With my close colleague Jean Singer, I interviewed a hundred successful men and women, focusing not on how their networks promote performance but on how they promote well-being. In particular, we focused on the role of relationships in promoting physical health; enabling growth inside and outside of work; providing a source of purpose and meaning; and creating a foundation of resilience to both large and small setbacks.

We began each interview asking people to tell us about a time in their lives when they were becoming more physically healthy. We acknowledged that due to the demands of job and home, health waxes and wanes as one moves through a career. What we were interested in exploring was a stretch where things were moving in what they considered to be a positive direction. Some spoke about times of improving fitness, some about losing weight, some about improved nutrition, some about preventive care (such as sleep), and some about managing blood pressure and stress through mindfulness initiatives. What Singer and I probed for was not what the individual did but rather the role of relationships in this stretch of life.

Let me tell you a few stories from this work.

Seth grew up in an idyllic town at the base of the Rockies. He was an avid athlete through school and was captain of a highly competitive basketball team in his senior year as well as a member of the varsity tennis team. Beyond this, Seth was always outside hiking or skiing, depending on the time of year. Exercise, activity, and good health were in his and his family's DNA.

Accepted into a well-regarded college, Seth was able to maintain his physical activity through the intramural basketball league and occasional ski trips with friends. He surrounded himself with a healthy group and excelled both athletically and academically. Coming out of school, he accepted a job at a highly regarded consulting firm and moved to Chicago. "Two things started at this point," he said. "First, the work hours and travel ballooned to a point where I was only able to get to a gym a couple of times a week. Second, the weather was horrible compared to what I was used to in Colorado. Between these two factors I began to fall out of sports and activities I had always enjoyed."

Life was not all bad, of course. Seth met a wonderful woman. They married, bought a starter home, had two children, then bought a better home in a school district they felt was best for their family. Given the demands of life and work, they decided to specialize in their roles. Seth focused more on the career front. "And all of this slowly eroded my condition and activity," he said. "We generally maintained good nutrition, but all exercise fell off, and the groups I had been a part of were way in the rearview. I actually tried at one point to join a community basketball league, but I was so out of shape that I twisted an ankle, and this persistent injury led me to fall out of most other forms of exercise for almost seven years."

Once he became strong enough, Seth joined a church basketball league. Without realizing it, he found himself in a situation where continued, consistent involvement was a priority, because the physical activity was embedded in social connections. He loved the camaraderie of his teammates, and he was aware that if he didn't show up, they might not have enough players for a team. He didn't mind the social pressure to be there, and he loved creating friendships and rebuilding his skills.

Seth took things one step further to ensure success. "I made Thursdays from 9–11 p.m. sacred," he said. "I told my EA, 'You can fly me anywhere you want, any time, but have me home for basketball at this time.'" Seth created what I call *stickiness* with this activity. He leveraged his EA to help hold him accountable and to keep work requests in perspective. His family members were motivated to hold him accountable for attending practices and games, because they were aware that "I would become grumpy when I did not go," he said.

Seth successfully absorbed basketball into his routine, and this led to his taking better care of himself when he was on the road. He wanted to be physically able to play and avoid injury, so he was much more likely to work out in the hotel gyms, eat a little better, and avoid the second glass of wine. All because he wanted to be there for his friends and show up in the best shape he could. These friends became more than basketball to him. He went on biking trips with two of them, and one was a part of his daughter's wedding. This is something that too many health-related programs miss. Programs like Weight Watchers create accountability groups that keep us from negative behaviors, and they often work for a while. But they rarely encourage the positive elements such as those that kept Seth involved in this activity.

Seth learned one more thing. He took his success from basketball and parlayed it into a second activity with tennis. This took him into new spheres of people who became friends and confidants. Tennis also deepened his relationship with his wife, whom he began to play doubles with. He wisely concluded our interview by letting us know: "Work adapts to life, if you let it."

Seth was one of many interviewees who pulled themselves out of their echo chambers by appealing to past skills. Others were successful by learning *new* skills. For example, one life-sciences executive described her foray this way: "I was the person who did everything possible to dodge gym in high school. I was OK until I hit my late thirties and finally got a rather stern warning from my doctor on exercise." She started walking around a nearby park at specific times and fell in with a group. "That was key, as it made it more enjoyable. We would share challenges in our work and lives, and it was fab for me because they came from such different perspectives than the people I spent time with at work." Group members began to set goals on how long they would walk, and eventually this moved to jogging and their first charity run. Fast-forward over a decade, and this executive now plans vacations with her husband around marathons they run together, accompanied by people from this initial group and other people she has become close to through running.

"The people were critical," she said. "And not just because they made me a little more accountable to show up. It is the depth of the connection. These people have seen me at my worst. They encouraged me on, and I have done the same." This executive's narrative contains a critical truism about situating the activity in relationships: these efforts do not just create a social pressure to persist; they also result in new friendships, an ability to be authentic with others and to take on added dimensionality in your life. And because the people often come from varied backgrounds, the interactions shape our perspectives on how we look at our own lives, what we see as stressful, and what we suddenly become grateful for. That's a perspective we miss if we are constantly surrounded by similarly educated or accomplished people.

Not all the success stories were around group sports or heroic athletic accomplishments. Many were around nutrition and eating more healthily. Others were around weight-reduction goals. And still others centered on managing stress through mindfulness and preventive-care measures. In other words, these steps took many different forms. But the key to all was a shift in the social ecosystem of the unhealthy behavior. Perhaps no story revealed this as clearly as Susan's.

The story of Susan, a manager at a research organization, shows how engaging in personal networks can help an individual break negative cycles and create deliberate life shifts. It wasn't until after her divorce, when she started seeing a new group of friends, that she was able to move away from the unhealthy patterns that had been increasing her stress and depleting her energy. Having met a new life partner who shares her values and aspirations, Susan now engages regularly with her new friendship group, and they push each other to be better on both personal and professional levels. Part of that is encouraging good nutrition.

In the bad old days, her ex-husband would encourage her to "just pick up Burger King on the way home" after a tiring day at work, "so we would eat a lot of fast food," she said. "And the group of friends we were hanging out with were sort of the same way. That was their instinct." Today, her significant other and her friends support her desire to eat more healthily. "That support system is real," she said.

Her group of friends encouraged her to move to a home closer to her job, which gave her greater opportunities for walking. This morphed into long walking meetings. She lost fifteen pounds and improved her connections to people at work. Her new friends and her improved work relationships have greatly enhanced her life. "I know I have the right support system," she said. "If I'm sick, I can stay out of work for three days, and everything will be fine. Those connections and my network will help take care of whatever will fall down on my end." (See the Coaching Break, "Crafting a Healthy Social Ecosystem.")

Shield from the Negative by Managing Micro-Stressors Intentionally

"OK. So that was a time when you sustained a positive trajectory of health. Now let's back up a moment. Can you tell me what got you into trouble to begin with? In other words, what led you to the point of poor health where you had to take concerted action?" Singer and I would typically ask this question about thirty minutes into the well-being interviews. Up to that point, we had been celebrating only the positives— the ways in which the interviewees had sustained trajectories of good health and the role of connections in that process. My question about an earlier, unhealthy time often caused people to pause and reflect deeply.

"Just life, I guess," or some variant, was the most common answer. Singer and I would continue to probe into that time period, always hoping to find common themes—a nasty boss, an unreasonable client, an impossible workload, an obsession with monetary success, a quest to outpace others. To be sure, we did hear some of that, but most people's reality was defined by something else, what we have come to call *relationship-based micro-stressors*. The real enemy was not one big challenge or obstacle but rather a never-ending barrage of small items that crowded out exercise, eating well, and sleep.

While relationships are critical sources of well-being, they also have the potential to multiply our stress. Think of a recent conference call in which you disagreed or sensed a disagreement, but the misalignment went unspoken; or you noticed for the third time in a week that a team member really needed coaching; or there was something worrying about a text message that you got from your child. We endure these micro-stressors throughout the day, often without ever being able to put our finger on what is hurting our well-being.

Broadly speaking, relationships create stress for us in three ways: they *drain our personal capacity*, *deplete our emotional reserves*, and *challenge our values or identity*. Let's look at each of these.

COACHING BREAK

Crafting a Healthy Social Ecosystem

We have all seen the surges in our gyms on January 1, only to see them empty out by January 30. Or perhaps we have made our own resolutions around diet or exercise that fade quickly, despite our good intentions. The research shows that the more-enduring shifts occur as a product of situating an activity in networks and—ideally—sharing a goal with others. Key positive relational elements are critical to long-term persistence. This is a very different approach from the conventional focus on mere accountability.

Step 1. Identify one or two health-related objectives, such as stress reduction, weight loss, or better fitness.

Objective 1 _____

Objective 2 _____

Step 2. Share those goals with other people. Informing others helps you maintain your commitment.

Person 1 _____

Person 2 _____

Step 3. Identify specific activities that will help you meet those objectives—for example, resuming an old skill, learning a new one, or joining charity walks.

Activity 1 _____

Activity 2 _____

Step 4. Identify positive relational elements that will create accountability and keep you going on those activities. These might include a walking buddy, a weight-loss partner, or a pickleball group.

Relational element 1 _____

Relational element 2 _____

Step 5. Make commitments to build deeper, more-trusting, more-authentic connections in those positive relationships, and create space for people from different walks of life to pull you into being someone new. Such commitments might include joining an effort toward a challenging goal or making time to connect with people after an activity rather than rushing home. Let people see you when you're vulnerable; talk about a wide range of topics and life experiences.

Commitment 1 _____

Commitment 2 _____

Step 6. Create a supportive ecosystem around these objectives, activities, and elements. For example, create "stickiness" at work by setting aside sacred times for your activities; have your assistant schedule healthy activities for you; surround yourself with supportive people outside work.

Ecosystem element 1 _____

Ecosystem element 2 _____

Drains on our personal capacity

The need to collaborate as part of our daily work has become standard in virtually every profession. We work hard to keep colleagues in the loop, we seek input and support from others, we are added to—and seldom dropped from—cc lists. All of this, of course, comes with ever-escalating productivity expectations. Beyond the "deliverables" that drain us, there are unspoken inefficiencies that arise from the way we work together. These collaboratively complex times create stress when they generate work or reduce our ability to do what we already have on our plate.

The micro-stressors that diminish our ability to complete our work and drain our personal capacity include surges in responsibilities and inefficient norms around email and other forms of communication; subpar performance from colleagues and supervisees; and unpredictable bosses. Most of us would be quick to cite these factors as stress points. But one that you might not have considered is misalignment of roles and priorities.

In today's workplace, the bulk of work is done through teams, and performance hinges on effective collaboration inside the team and beyond. As a result, we all experience a lot more misalignment than we realize. A functional counterpart of yours announces that her group is starting a task, but your group is already working on that, so you have to schedule a meeting to clarify who is doing what. Or tension rises as team members emphasize their functional contributions over the team's mission or align with incentives from their home units, setting up competing priorities.

We may be fully aware that these invisible relational issues need to be figured out and dealt with, but most of the time we just don't have the bandwidth. In today's work environments, people are scattered across so many teams that there is no time for anyone to engage in effective team development. So teams continue to lurch from issue to issue, misalignment continues to drain our personal capacity, and there is a constant and growing hum of stress.

Depletion of our emotional reserves

These reserves help us counteract difficult feelings and negative in-teractions, such as worry about people we're close to, uncertainty over the impact of our actions, fear of repercussions, and simply feeling de-energized by certain types of interactions. While my research shows a significant performance impact from positive, energizing interactions, I have found that the effect of negative ties—those that de-energize us or create mistrust or fear—is even more important to attend to. Negative connections, ranging from people who harbor hidden agendas that are at odds with their stated motivations, to individuals who don't deliver what they promise, to teammates who can't admit to their limitations, are typically only a small portion of our network interactions, but their effect can be significant. For example, when people have hidden agen-das, "it's really draining because you're never quite sure where they're coming from," said Zack, a senior scientist with a biotech firm. Even if negative interactions are brief, they can leave a footprint of worry that lasts for hours or even days.

Management itself—just being a manager, with responsibility for others' success and well-being—can seriously drain our emotional re-serves. None of us wants to be seen as a "bad" boss. We want to do the right thing for people, but often we feel limited in being able to provide subordinates with sufficient time and attention, the tools and training to be successful, or the rewards and recognition to feel appreciated. We have to manage performance issues, give critical feedback, resolve group conflicts, and, in unfortunate circumstances, have confronta-tional conversations and even fire people. Handling these situations in a way that is simultaneously constructive, empathic, and moral can push us past our emotional limits.

Gerhard, a biotech manager who is responsible for about two thou-sand people, described the constant concern he felt as he led his group through a reorganization: "Everyone's going to go through substantial change in the next four to five years. How do I get them through the change curve? Is everyone being supported in the right way? Are we communicating in the right way? How do I get through this reorganization effectively with the team and for the team? That's where my angst comes from." Behind Gerhard's stress lies a fear that he'll fall short, that he won't get it right and will let his people down. "What information do you let people know and when? Everyone has a different opinion about how to do that. And sometimes I have to mediate differing opinions between management versus my leadership team. If it were just up to me and I was in a bubble, it would be less stressful."

Fear can have a profound effect on our experience of stress. Some people create fear through their dictatorial styles. Others are fearmongers who see and experience fear in a broad number of interactions, often where it simply does not exist. These people make things worse, not better.

Anxious leaders can also create chain reactions of stress that reverberate down the hierarchy. When an overloaded leader is unavailable for guidance or decision-making, the stress passes onto their subordinates. We get two-line emails that launch us into action, and we start working without really knowing whether we're on the right path. Secondhand stress also occurs when, as a result of overload, leaders make snap judgments without taking the time to delve into the issues. We're left trying to figure out whether to follow their lead or push back. Leaders may also pass on their stress by tone of voice, impatience, or body language—a transmission of a negative emotional state that can trigger us to feel likewise.

Challenges to our values or identity

Most of us would like to think that the values and sense of identity that guide our actions, both at work and home, are solid and fixed, but often they are more susceptible to influence than we realize.

Have you ever felt pressure to do things that didn't feel entirely right? For example, if you deal with clients, have you felt pressured to meet "the numbers" by pushing expensive pricing rather than aim for client satisfaction? Have you been told to fire someone who had been a faithful contributor for decades? How about pressure to be all in, meaning available 24-7 regardless of the needs of your personal life?

Every week, people face many such moments that chip away at their values and sense of identity—moments that nudge them from being the person who always stands up for what's right to becoming the person who does what's expedient because it's better in the long run for the career, or it's just how life is. These moments don't come with neon signs saying "Warning: This decision will change how you see yourself!" Instead they sneak up on us, and often they come and go before we realize what has happened. But over time, they can lead us far away from what we truly value.

Throughout my interviews, I heard many successful people describe stark moments when they realized they had spent years in pursuit of goals that were misaligned with who they were when they started their careers. And these were the lucky ones. Many of us never have these moments of revelation. Instead we toil along, sensing on some deep level that our lives have become inconsistent with our values and identity. As this disconnect between who we are and what we stand for continues to grow, it takes a toll in stress, which gets worse if we start to feel self-doubt for not pushing back harder.

Identifying and acting on systemic micro-stressors

Stress, of course, is not unique to today. What is unique is the quantity, rate, and variety of these micro-stressors and how they come to us through relationships in so many forms. They are part of the rhythm of our work lives, and we take them as a normal cost of doing business. So they rarely rise to the level of deliberate examination and action.

Traditional advice on coping with negative or stressful interactions doesn't work in this domain, because micro-stressors are deeply embedded in accepted ways of working together. They come at us through interactions that are too numerous and high velocity to handle one by one. Have you ever tried to take just one micro-stressor, such as a colleague who missed the mark on a joint project or the emotional toll from the departure of a trusted work colleague, and explain it to someone close to you? Often these discussions are helpful for processing and managing the stress, but it can take twenty or thirty minutes just to describe the history, dependencies, and context so your listener can empathize and possibly make helpful suggestions, which (if that even happens) might take an additional half-hour. We might have time for one of these per day or per week, but we are getting hit with twenty to thirty micro-stressors a day. Who has time to articulate this all? And who, on the receiving end, wants to hear it?

Micro-stressors pose a different dilemma than we have seen before, so we need new approaches for dealing with them. (See the Coaching Break, "Identifying Your Micro-Stressors.") The table there will help you identify two to three micro-stressors that have a persistent impact on your life. Micro-stressors create an emotional buildup that needs to be released before you can think rationally about a constructive response, so it often helps to first undertake an activity, such as exercise, time with family, or a favorite hobby, that helps you decompress. You're then in a position to reflect on and process your stressors.

The true source of stress can get lost in the noise of anxiety or defensiveness, and conversations with others can help you unpack what's really bothering you and why. One leader facing a work situation that almost drove her to leave her job found that sitting down with a trusted colleague helped her diagnose what the issue really was. "I remember at the time just feeling really frustrated," she said. "And I couldn't exactly unpack where the frustration was coming from. Was it just the pressure? And, ultimately, through the questions that she asked, I was like, 'You're right. It's because I don't feel like I'm having the space to contribute what I'm capable of.'" Pinpointing the problem enabled her to engage in a dialogue with her boss and relieve the tensions.

But calling out the micro-stressors that have the greatest impact on you is easy compared with the two other activities in the "Identifying Your Micro-Stressors" coaching break: reflecting on micro-stressors that you create for others and those that you are unnecessarily magnifying.

Most of us don't want to be sources of stress, but the reality is that when we collaborate, we inevitably throw micro-stressors at others all the time. We don't quite get all our work done by the deadline. We prioritize our personal goals over the group's. We send those late-night emails. We make a cutting or unfair comment at breakfast that sours our spouse's entire day. We undermine a colleague's self-confidence. And on and on. I'm not saying that you need to be perfect; I'm only asking that you think about the micro-stressors you perpetrate, as a perspective-building activity.

Another perspective-building activity is asking yourself where you are needlessly magnifying your micro-stressors. Is it really *that* big a deal that someone didn't deliver reliably or prioritizes her own goals over the team's? Could you ignore those late-night emails? Could you let a family member's unfair remark just roll off your back? Could you learn to be immune to confidence-busting comments?

Add Dimensionality to Life through Interactions That Generate Purpose

If we are able to tackle two or three micro-stressors proactively, what do we do with the rest? One solution is to keep them in perspective. Mindfulness practices, such as meditation or gratitude journaling, can be helpful. And, of course, maintaining physical health through exercise is probably the most important lever we have for combating stress. But there are also important relational solutions: people who have greater dimensionality in their lives and broader connections just don't experience micro-stressors in the same way. They have a greater tendency to keep them in perspective rather than magnify them through rumination or conversations with others.

I equate this to a scenario most are familiar with. Have you ever had something traumatic happen that instantly changed the way you thought about all the little inconveniences and annoyances in your life, and made you wonder why you had been so consumed by them? Experiences like

COACHING BREAK

Identifying Your Micro-Stressors

First, indicate two or three micro-stressors that have the greatest impact on you at present. Place an X in the appropriate cells to identify the source(s) of each. Focus on those you can take action on. Then take a second pass through the table and reflect on micro-stressors that *you are creating for others*. Place a Y in those cells. Finally, in a third pass through the table, reflect on micro-stressors that *you are unnecessarily magnifying*—points where you need to learn to keep things in perspective a little better. Place an O in these cells. Think about how you can act on your top micro-stressors and de-escalate the others.

Sources of stress

What is driving your stress?	Boss	Other leaders	Peers	Clients	Team	Loved ones
Who is driving your stress?						
Micro-stressors draining your personal capacity						
Misalignment of roles or priorities						
When others don't deliver reliably						
Unpredictable behavior from a person in a position of authority						
Volume and diversity of collaborative demands						
Surge in responsibilities at work or home						

What is driving your stress?	Who is driving your stress?					
	Boss	Other leaders	Peers	Clients	Team	Loved ones
Micro-stressors depleting your emotional reserves						
Managing and feeling responsibility for the success and well-being of others						
Confrontational conversations						
Mistrust in your network						
People who spread a contagion of stress						
Political maneuvering by boss or peers						
Micro-stressors challenging your identity						
Pressure to pursue goals that are out of sync with your personal values						
When someone undermines your sense of self-confidence, worth, or control						
Negative or draining interactions with family (direct or extended) and friends						
Disruptions to your network						

this shift our perspective and help us to see the small items for what they truly are: small. I am convinced that—without the need for trauma—people who manage dimensionality experience micro-stressors this way. They are able to laugh or shake their heads over small things. Their identity and existence is not challenged in the same way.

Well-being is clearly tied to a sense of purpose—in essence, a belief that life is meaningful and serves aims higher than yourself. People with a strong sense of purpose in life tend to do better on a range of measures of physical health, psychological health, longevity, and overall well-being. Sense of purpose has been related to a reduction in cardio-vascular disease. In one study, a one-point increase on a six-point scale measuring purpose in life corresponded to a 27 percent decreased risk of having a heart attack among people with heart disease. For older adults, a one-point difference in purpose translated to a 22 percent decreased risk of stroke.[4] A sense of purpose can work to reduce stress. A study of 6,840 teachers found that individuals with a greater sense of purpose in life were better at managing stress and had better self-rated health status.[5] Having a sense of purpose has been linked to better sleep, lower risk of dementia, and lower risk of depression.[6] People with higher purpose in life tend to engage in healthier behaviors such as exercising more and availing themselves of preventive health services, leading to better overall health.[7]

Interactions with others can create a sense of purpose by helping us find our higher aspirations, feel part of something larger than ourselves, and connect on meaningful grounds. Connecting with others who share values or care about similar outcomes helps build purpose. So does work-ing with energizers—people who leave you feeling enthused and moti-vated. Energizers, who often talk about the "why" of the work and what is possible rather than focusing on the demands or the negatives, can contribute to our sense of purpose. The flip side is that de-energizers can drain us of our motivation and sense of value in the work we do. As people experience interactions with energizers and others who help them see that their efforts have meaning, they bring themselves more fully to their work. Negative or draining interactions may remain, but they seem more manageable or balanced if we have a few purposeful relationships at work.[8]

Throughout my interviews, I would routinely hear people who appeared to have it all describe how demanding and difficult their lives were. But, like clockwork, I would encounter one in ten people who would tell a different story: they enjoyed the positives of being high performers, but they also lived life a little more on their terms. Their day-to-day lives were busy, but they were less reactive, and they more effectively shaped their realities at work and at home. The key difference for these people lay with the breadth and dimensionality in their networks.

The critical role of life anchors

These people—whom I call ten percenters—generally had life anchors that ensured that they did not let themselves become too unidimensional. The anchors took three forms: *life roles*, *process orientation*, and *value anchors*.

LIFE ROLES. Impose structure through role clarity, connections, and rituals (such as journaling) that shape life and connections, rather than letting systemic pressures take over. For example, more than twenty years ago, just as his career was at a major inflection point, Philip, a senior leader in the software world, had an epiphany. While he was sitting in a rocking chair on a porch in North Carolina, he suddenly realized that if he took the next logical step in his career—a step that would have been the natural outcome of his decades of work and that would have been considered a dream job by most people—he would be unable to live the way he wanted. He spent three hours that day clarifying, with his wife, the experiences and contributions he wanted to make with his life and boiled these down to six roles. He saw that he was and wanted to continue to be a "natural being," meaning a person who respects the body's need for sleep, healthy food, and exercise. He also wanted to continue to be an organizational pioneer, a good friend, a good family member, a global citizen, and a "spiritual being."

Each of these roles translates into specific actions that he takes and groups that he engages with. Every week he journals on how he has fulfilled and made progress in these roles, and he adjusts his plans for the next week on the basis of where he needs to invest time. Every morning, he journals his hopes for the day, keeping some or all of these roles in mind. "It is amazing to me how often just writing things down seems to almost make them happen somehow in the day," he said. As you can imagine, he has accumulated stacks of journals over the years. The roles form an anchor for him to plan how he is living and who he is engaging with.

This process allows him to put structure into his life and helps him prevent work from taking over. Philip is quicker than anyone I know to choose not to do things that don't align with his roles. And most people respect the heck out of him for living life this way. I have known Philip for twenty years, and he always manages to come out on top with fantastic jobs but also a life that most can only envy.

PROCESS ORIENTATION. People who fall into the process-orientation category tend to have heuristics for embracing the moment with other people. They are more likely to see life as emergent and to cherish time with others. What is cool about these people is their ability to lean into the flow of a situation. For example, rather than define who they want to have dinner with, and spend weeks trying to align calendars, they might simply tell a large group that they are going to dinner and ask whether anyone wants to come.

In a range of subtle ways, they work with the flow of life and lean into relationships and experiences more than most people would think possible. They capitalize on micro-moments to expand their connections and grow, they embrace moments fully, and they take opportunities as they arise. "I am a chronic learner," one executive said to me. "I have an old house built in the seventeenth century, so I spend a lot of time working on that and spend a lot of time talking to people about that. I am a novice sailor and enjoy sailing through a yacht club I belong to. I enjoy gardening, so I am active in our gardening clubs. I teach two classes a term. I am actively involved as the president of my alumni association. I keep in touch with friend groups from all stages of life, and I now run a barbecue that brings all of these people together and has become a four-day event." Like others who have adopted a process orientation, this person fully embraces chance micro-moments as they arise, capitalizing on them to expand his connections and grow, and using them to move forward, often in surprising new directions.

VALUE ANCHORS. These are anchors that people cultivate through life experiences. They are less holistic than the first two, but provide nonnegotiable points that people tend to form connections around and through which they create dimensionality. One common value anchor is faith—for example, as a way to develop a sense of self in the universe or as a channel to help the underprivileged. Others include spending time with family, whether direct or extended; spending time with friends—really prioritizing time with them and being present for them; and volunteering, which includes serving as a role model.

To keep work in perspective—her company is in the midst of an acquisition—Lanie leans heavily on a mentor and friend in another division, as well as her husband and a close circle of friends. She said:

> The acquisition is complicated. The day-to-day work is complicated. I lost my quality director at a crucial time leading up to a quality audit. We've had issues with a supplier. Our financials are good, but the other divisions are struggling, so I feel that weight. I'm Type A and push myself and others pretty hard, but I'm clear on my purpose: to make the business better and do it in a way that brings other people and teams with me. Plenty of people can make the business better for the short term, but nobody wants to work for them. So I'm honest with my leadership team about my values and priorities. I'm also clear that work doesn't define me or dictate everything—my husband, my kids, and my church family keep me grounded in what matters most.

Lanie's work demands are global and the hours are long, but she focuses on the positive side of 24/7 connectivity. "It goes both ways," she said. "I can view work as interrupting my family life, or I can take advantage and unapologetically integrate it all. I can be at a kid's event and respond to a text or email. I usually spend a couple of hours early in the morning doing focused work, but otherwise I appreciate the ability to be where I need to be and know people can reach me. I also have to check myself: How do I give the most value, not necessarily give the most time?" She meets with her assistant every Friday for a calendar review, looking two to three weeks out. "We move things around, say no or delegate things that other people can do, and make sure I have built in blocks of time for longer-term goals. Those things can fall off easily if I'm not proactive."

Beyond life anchors

Our sense of purpose in life is deeply constructed through interactions we have inside and outside of work. In my research, I have consistently seen that organizations doing noble work—curing cancer, saving children's lives, eradicating disease—can be among the unhappiest, while those doing seemingly mundane things can be the most engaged.

Purpose is not just in the nature of our work but also in the networks around the work. Two broad spheres of connections generate a sense of purpose for most people:

Work-defined connections

- *Leaders/culture*. Working for an inspiring leader or vision or being part of a culture that does the right things and/or cares about colleagues' success.

- *Peers*. Co-creating or cascading a meaningful future and/or engaging those with similar values authentically.

- *Team/mentor*. Mentoring and creating a context for others to thrive—helping, seeing growth, sharing your learning, being transparent and vulnerable.

- *Consumer/stakeholder*. Validation from consumers of output—products that improve life, for example.

Life-defined connections

- *Spirituality*. Interactions around religion, music, art, poetry, and other aesthetic spheres of life that put work in a broader context.

- *Civic/volunteer*. Contributing to meaningful groups creates a wellness benefit from giving and brings you in contact with diverse but like-minded people.

- *Friends/community*. Often forged through collective activity such as athletic endeavors or book or dinner clubs.

- *Family*. Caring for family and modeling valued behaviors as well as maintaining identity through interactions with extended family.

Shift one activity to yield more purpose

Far too often people tell me: "I don't have time for these interactions that will generate purpose. My job is too demanding. My work does not allow me time to engage in this way." The list goes on. But the consistent theme is that these people are treating work and life as a trade-off. They are not looking for the synergies they can get from adapting small activities to lead to a greater sense of purpose in these spheres.

To see how a successful individual engages in activities that allow for multiple touchpoints of purpose, consider Juliet, whose promotion to head of product development for her tech company has taken her far beyond the world of research that was her original training ground. The job is intense, but she finds dimensionality outside of work through volunteering, family, and her community of friends.

Much of her volunteering happens in the context of her children's school. As busy as she is at work, she still spends time working for the school. She and her husband go to the school "a ridiculous amount of time—some days it feels like we live there, even more than the kids do."

It was clear to me how Juliet's volunteering dovetailed with one of her other purpose-related anchors, family, but I was surprised at how it also connected with the value that she places on friends and community. "A lot of the people that I consider my closest friends are people I've met through the school," Juliet said. "These are the people I like to hang out with socially anyway."

Or consider Eric, who demonstrates that a single activity can drive multiple sources of purpose. In Eric's case, the activity was connecting with colleagues to change his workplace's "pizza culture"—there was pizza at virtually every meeting, and a pizza party at 4 p.m. every day. This was painful for Eric, who had grown up in France and for whom thoughtful cooking, eating, and sharing mealtimes was an ingrained part of his culture.

Eric connected with the company's leaders to make the case that the workplace needed to be a healthier environment for employees and that supporting broad aspects of employees' lives should be emphasized as a company value. He challenged the leaders to have the courage to change the company's entrenched culture.

He connected with peers, co-creating ideas for a new workplace culture and engaging others with values similar to his, and he connected with his nonwork community by sourcing healthier foods from a nearby fruit and vegetable market. "I started interacting with all those people, and we turned the situation around," he said. Gradually the workplace culture shifted—people became more aware of what and when they ate, and there was an increased emphasis on healthy behaviors, such as walking outside and taking the stairs. (See the Coaching Break, "Shift Activity to Optimize Purpose.")

Principles to drive purpose: be intentional in small moments

Look to engage more purposefully in small moments. Anchor this from values within and focus on how to shape, rather than be shaped by, all the interactions coming at you.

Live micro-moments intentionally—show intentionality in all of the small moments. Believe in people, lift them up; help them do the right thing; uncover commonalities; understand aspirations. Simply altering the way we engage in existing relations often uncovers ways our existing networks can fuel a sense of purpose.

Create a persistent dialogue on what is worth doing. People who avoid crisis moments in life spend more time talking with others about ways to live life. One successful executive formed a board of people who showed up in life as she wanted to. Rather than being a traditional advisory group of mentors, this group was younger and older and from all walks of life but helped her consistently reflect on how she was engaging with purpose.

Return to relationships, often forged by fire through difficult situations. How you handle adverse moments with others—seeing possibilities, being proactive, commiserating to some degree but not too much—gets you through but also builds connections that you go back to.

Lean into transitions to experience purpose

A final lesson from our successful people is to see transitions not as threats but as opportunities to discover a new and better version of yourself. Look to see and unplug from things that are draining purpose and invest in new activities that slingshot you into groups you want to engage with as part of your identity—and then stick it out.

Consider a very successful high-tech executive who, over a twenty-year career, had become someone she had not planned to be. The job's toll on her health and identity slowly burned her out, and she quit a job that many would envy. She was determined to lean into her health. Although she prides herself on her skepticism, she decided to give yoga a try. She promised her husband she would try it three times before giving up.

The first time, she rolled her eyes at the overly nice people who showed up. The second time, she internally mocked the "flaky" and "granola" instructor. The third time, she endured a little better but nevertheless felt she was done. As the class ended, the instructor walked around the room and touched every person on the head.

COACHING BREAK

Shift Activity to Optimize Purpose

Reflect on the figure below, which will help you to prioritize the work-defined and life-defined connections described earlier in this chapter. First, allocate 100 points to the spheres that currently provide you

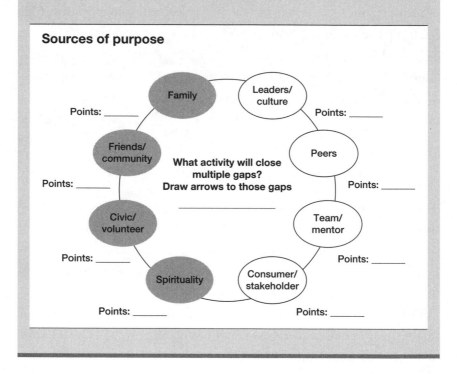

To my friend's deep surprise, she burst into tears. As she unpacked this, she realized that this was the first time she had let herself be vulnerable or authentic in a long time. Falling out of pose. Exhausted from what looked easy. And sharing this vulnerability with strangers in the room. This was not something that her corporate persona would have tolerated.

with a sense of purpose. Distribute more points to those that provide an exceptionally high sense of purpose and fewer points to those
that provide less of a sense of purpose. Allocating zero points to one
or more spheres is OK. Review your allocation of points to identify
spheres that you would like to better connect with to add dimensionality to your life.

Second, in the middle of the circle, indicate one activity that you
currently engage in—maybe exercise, music, community service, or
spiritual pursuits—that, if you shifted slightly, could have the greatest impact on the largest number of spheres and draw arrows to the
spheres that this activity would affect. If this is not immediately obvious
to you, think about interests from your past. Leaning back into athletic
pursuits, hobbies, and passions is often the first step for entrenched
people to slingshot into new groups. Simple shifts to include different
spheres of people in your pursuit of these activities can often magnify
purpose. Rather than pursue a 10K running goal in isolation, consider
running with your child, the child's friend, and the friend's parent as a
way to lean into a larger group.

Then create "stickiness": commit to a goal with this group, set hard
rules, and engage family or friends in reinforcing your pursuit. Con-
solidate the shift into your life and then do it once or twice more—it is
amazing how work adapts to life if you let it.

Flash forward, and yoga has become a central component of her and
her husband's life. It defines a large portion of their social world and
even their vacations. This never would have materialized without her
leaning into and persisting through a transition. It wasn't so much the
yoga as the relationships formed through the activity that mattered.
They added dimensionality and perspective to her life that had not

been there when work ruled all. They became a source of resilience. And they helped give her courage to live life on her terms rather than others' definitions of success.

Most of us experience large portions of life on autopilot. But growth happens in moments when you either capitalize on an emergent opportunity or initiate a shift. Consider some insights:

- *Initiate transition when it makes no sense.* The time to stretch is when you are comfortable or when you feel you need to hunker down to get through a situation. Instead, lean in. Surge into a transition, reaching out early and broadly and reestablishing connections into existing activities you enjoy (faith or sports) and initiating at least one new one activity.

- *Focus on your aspirational self, behaviors, and relationships.* Use transitions to reflect on socially defined goals and aspirations that have shaped you. Reflect on one way to invest in work that you want to be doing or one activity with others that would add dimensionality and breadth to your life.

- *Beware of shocks or surges that pull you away from your values.* Don't let your reaction to a negative moment or stretch of time take you away from who you want to be. Too often, what seems temporary becomes embedded in expectations around you.

We live in challenging times, to be sure. But our experience is often of our own making. Never in history have we had a greater ability to shape what we do and with whom. Don't give up this control.

. . .

In chapter 2, we saw that successful collaboration is part of an infinite loop, which is repeated in figure 8-1.

On the left side, you play offense in addressing collaboration overload by challenging your beliefs, imposing structures that shield you from unnecessary collaborative demands, and adapting behaviors that

FIGURE 8-1

The infinite loop

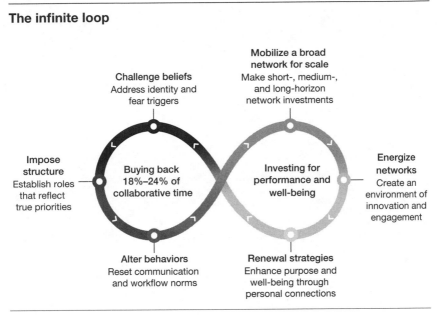

Challenge beliefs
Address identity and
fear triggers

Mobilize a broad
network for scale
Make short-, medium-,
and long-horizon
network investments

Impose
structure
Establish roles
that reflect
true priorities

Buying back
18%–24% of
collaborative time

Investing for
performance and
well-being

Energize
networks
Create an
environment of
innovation and
engagement

Alter behaviors
Reset communication
and workflow norms

Renewal strategies
Enhance purpose and
well-being through
personal connections

ensure efficiencies. On the right side, you engage in strategies for drawing on personal connections to become a more effective performer, achieve scale, and increase your well-being.

I hope that by now you can see—and really feel—that this is not just some abstract board game, that the infinite loop is real, and all of these elements are interdependent. Each side of the loop reinforces the other: the strategies on the left side create time, space, and courage to take actions that improve effectiveness and well-being. The strategies on the right side yield greater performance and reputation, which in turn help you engage in higher-value collaborations and further improve your performance.

As you become more proactive, and as you grow into the skill of shaping your work, rather than letting it shape you, you can truly free yourself from the work culture that demands *more, more, more* of your time and energy. Instead, you can focus on bringing more to your life in a holistic sense: *more* to your deepest work-related passions, *more* to your family, *more* to your friends—and *more* to yourself.

NOTES

Chapter 1

1. Confidentiality agreements and my own obligation to protect the privacy of the people I interviewed prevent me from saying exactly where Scott—not his real name—worked and what product he worked on. But I'm drawing on my research to create a composite story that will give you a feel for the kind of work he did, without divulging any secrets. That is an MO I will use throughout this book—I will tap my research to create composite, fictional examples that accurately represent the findings I derived from real people in real companies.

Chapter 5

1. Margaret J. Peterson, *Hoosier Times*, online obituary, August 25, 2019, https://www.hoosiertimes.com/herald_times_online/obituaries/margaret-peterson-88 /article_7492a8e3-bcb2-5f82-8a3b-e787a6a7b623.html, accessed April 20, 2020.

2. Kevin Dutton, *The Wisdom of Psychopaths: What Saints, Spies, and Serial Killers Can Teach Us about Success* (New York: Scientific American/Farrar, Straus and Giroux, 2012), 109, fn.

3. Cyril Couffe and George A. Michael, "Failures Due to Interruptions or Distractions: A Review and a New Framework," *American Journal of Psychology* 130, no. 2 (2017): 163–181.

4. Kristin Wong, "How Long It Takes to Get Back on Track After a Distraction," Lifehacker, July 29, 2015, https://lifehacker.com/how-long-it-takes-to-get-back-on-track-after-a-distract-1720708353, accessed April 20, 2020.

5. Gloria Mark, Daniela Gudith, and Ulrich Klocke, "The Cost of Interrupted Work: More Speed and Stress," Proceedings of the 2008 Conference on Human Factors in Computing Systems, 2008, conference paper, Florence, Italy.

Part Two

1. R. Cross and R. Thomas, "How Top Talent Uses Networks and Where Rising Stars Get Trapped," *Organizational Dynamics* 37 (2008): 165–180.

Chapter 6

1. Ronald S. Burt, *Structural Holes: The Social Structure of Competition* (Cambridge, MA: Harvard University Press, 1992); Ronald S. Burt, "The Network Structure of Social Capital," in *Research in Organizational Behavior* 22, eds. Barry Staw and Robert Sutton (Greenwich, CT: JAI Press, 2000).

Chapter 7

1. For one efficient way to assess networks, see the Agility Accelerator application at www.robcross.org (click on "Propel Organizational Agility and Alignment").

2. Daniel Z. Levin and Rob Cross, "The Strength of Weak Ties You Can Trust: The Mediating Role of Trust in Effective Knowledge Transfer," *Management Science* 50, no. 11 (November 2004): 1477–1490.

Chapter 8

1. Heather Long, "The Unhappy States of America: Despite an Improving Economy, Americans Are Glum," *Washington Post*, March 30, 2018, https://www.washingtonpost.com/news/wonk/wp/2018/03/30/the-unhappy-states-of-america-despite-an-improving-economy-americans-are-glum/, accessed March 20, 2021.

2. J. S. House, K. R. Landis, and D. Umberson, "Social Relationships and Health," *Science* 241, no. 4865 (1988): 540–545.

3. N. A. Christakis and J. H. Fowler, *Connected* (New York: Hachette Book Group, 2009).

4. R. Cohen, C. Bavishi, and A. Rozanski, "Purpose in Life and Its Relationship to All-Cause Mortality and Cardiovascular Events: A Meta-analysis," *Psychosomatic Medicine* 78, no. 2 (2016): 122–133.

5. F. Li et al., "The Role of Stress Management in the Relationship between Purpose in Life and Self-rated Health in Teachers: A Mediation Analysis," *International Journal of Environmental Research and Public Health* 13, no. 7 (2016): 719.

6. D. Turner, C. E. Smith, and J. C. Ong, "Is Purpose in Life Associated with Less Sleep Disturbance in Older Adults?" *Sleep Science and Practice* 1, no. 14 (2017): 1–14; P. A. Boyle, A. S. Buchman, L. L. Barnes et al., "Effect of a Purpose in Life on Risk of Incident Alzheimer Disease and Mild Cognitive Impairment in Community-Dwelling Older Persons," *Archives of General Psychiatry* 67, no. 3 (2010): 304–310; A. Wood and S. Joseph, "The Absence of Positive Psychological (Eudemonic) Well-Being as a Risk Factor for Depression: A Ten-Year Cohort Study," *Journal of Affective Disorders* 122, no. 3 (2010): 213–217.

7. E. S. Kim and S. H. Konrath, "Volunteering Is Prospectively Associated with Health Care Use among Older Adults," *Social Science & Medicine* 149 (2016): 122–129.

8. R. Cross, W. Baker, and A. Parker, "What Creates Energy in Organizations?" *MIT Sloan Management Review*, Summer 2003.

INDEX

ACKNOWLEDGMENTS

My long list of heartfelt thanks begins with the Connected Commons, the consortium I cofounded as a way to help organizations participate in and stay up to date on network research.

The idea for this book goes back to when my colleagues and I were analyzing large networks within Commons member organizations and realized that individual employees and managers desperately needed new collaborative skills to thrive in an environment of ever-escalating work intensity. Once the idea for the book got rolling, member organizations supported the research in two vital ways: first, they provided tremendously valuable resources, allowing me to conduct massive quantitative network analyses and to interview more than five hundred executives in a series of qualitative studies. I am grateful to all those interviewees for letting me into their thoughts and experiences.

Just as important, the Commons organizations constantly challenged my thinking, pushing me to come up with insights that were not only academically interesting but also relevant to their struggling employees and managers. Practically every page of this book can be traced back to a conversation or an "Aha!" moment in a discussion with people connected to the Commons. I am aware that this kind of fruitful, long-term collaboration is exceedingly rare. Access to the Commons' resources and brain trust is a gift that goes beyond anything I ever anticipated when I began studying networks years ago.

Though there are far too many people in the Commons to call out by name (and I ask everyone's forgiveness for this), I would like to thank a number of individuals who have formed the inner working group of the

Commons over the years. Deb Zehner has provided tireless support to the Commons in many ways, big and small—her work has been central to its success—and to me as a researcher and writer. Her intellectual contributions underpin the chapters on collaborative overload. Similarly, Greg Pryor has been a nonstop source of intellectual contribution, creativity, and energy since day one of the Commons; many of the ideas in this book were shaped through countless weekend calls where we both found space to think and be creative.

Peter Amidon, Michael Arena, Mike Benson, Inga Carboni, Jim Carling, Arun Chidambaram, Sally Colella, Chris Ernst, Rebecca Garau, Peter Gray, Andrew Parker, Jean Singer, and David Sylvester have been similarly important to the evolution of this work through many, many interactions. My thanks also go to Beth Horowitz Steel, a partner at the strategy consulting and research firm Glenbrook Partners, for her insights into the payments industry, which helped in the drafting of chapter 1.

On an institutional level, I am deeply indebted to Babson College and many academic colleagues who see the value in rigorous applied research and have created space and support for this work. A wonderful set of corporate advisers has also provided a vibrant interface between the world of academia and practice and helped me focus my research on what matters most to people. In particular, I am extremely grateful for the partnership with the Institute for Corporate Productivity (i4cp) and the entire team there. Although there are too many to name, I would like to specifically thank Kevin Oakes for seeing the possibility in the partnership and Carrie Bevis, Kevin Osborne, and Erik Samdahl for their ceaseless efforts and their unflagging belief in this work. I would also like to thank the Innovation Resource Center for Human Resources (IRC4HR), and in particular Jodi Starkman and Hal Burlingame, for their belief in and support of early stages of this work.

Many thanks to the editorial team at Harvard Business Review Press. Melinda Merino was an enthusiastic supporter of the ideas, and my editor at the Press, Scott Berinato, did a wonderful job on idea development, editing, title, jacket design, and exhibit design. I am extremely thankful to Andy O'Connell for helping me integrate nearly two decades' worth of research into a rich and engaging format, and for his kind and tactful persistence in not letting me take the easier routes at various points in this process.

Most of all, I would like to thank my family. My wife, Deb, has been a constant source of inspiration and support throughout this work. Many of the core ideas in the book were developed in discussions with her. Deb, you are the best thing that has ever happened to me! Thanks also go to my son, Connor, and daughter, Rachel—you have kept me humble and grounded through constant chiding and have taught me a tremendous amount about what to value in relationships. If you are representative of the next generation, then we will all be much better off in the future.

ABOUT THE AUTHOR

ROB CROSS is the Edward A. Madden Professor of Global Leadership at Babson College and the cofounder and research director of the Connected Commons business consortium. For more than twenty years, he has studied the underlying networks of effective organizations and the collaborative practices of high performers. Working with more than three hundred organizations and reaching thousands of leaders from the front line to the C-suite, he has identified specific ways to cultivate vibrant, effective networks at all levels of an organization and any career stage.

He is a renowned thinker, writer, and speaker whose category-defying ideas, courses, and tools have influenced fields as diverse as organizational design, change, collaboration, teams, agility, innovation, and talent optimization. His network strategies for effective collaboration are transforming the way people lead, work, and live in a hyperconnected world.

He has authored six *Harvard Business Review* articles on practical approaches to enhancing collaboration. He is the coauthor of five books, including *The Hidden Power of Social Networks*. He can be reached at www.robcross.org.